Palm Springs Flavors

The Best of Desert Eating, with Recipes from the Area's Chefs

Text by

Henry Fenwick
&
Eric Wadlund

Photography by

Tony Tornay

Additional Scenic Photography by

Ren Navez

WESTCLIFFE PUBLISHERS
westcliffepublishers.com

International Standard Book Numbers:
ISBN-10: 1-56579-582-2
ISBN-13: 978-1-56579-582-2

Editor: Kelly Smith
Designer: CORVUS Design Studio and Publishing Services
Production Manager: Craig Keyzer

Published by:
Westcliffe Publishers, Inc.
P.O. Box 1261
Englewood, CO 80150

Printed in China by World Print, Ltd.

Library of Congress Cataloging-in-Publication Data:

Fenwick, Henry.
  Palm Springs flavors : the best of desert eating, with recipes from the area's chefs / text by
Henry Fenwick and Eric Wadlund ; photography by Tony Tornay and Ren Navez.
     p. cm.
  Includes index.
  ISBN-13: 978-1-56579-582-2
  ISBN-10: 1-56579-582-2
  1. Cookery, American--California style. 2. Cookery--California--Palm Springs.
3. Restaurants--California--Palm Springs. I. Wadlund, Eric. II. Title.
  TX715.2.C34.F46 2007
  641.59794--dc22   2006102223

*For more information about other fine books and calendars from Westcliffe Publishers, please contact your
local bookstore, call us at 1-800-523-3692, or visit us on the Web at* **westcliffepublishers.com.**

ACKNOWLEDGEMENTS

ERIC WADLUND AND I WOULD LIKE TO THANK THE MANY PEOPLE who have provided help and gave us encouragement as this book was in progress. First of all, of course, our extreme gratitude to the chefs who shared their recipes with us. Their generosity and kindness have been overwhelming.

Many people throughout the Coachella Valley have given us their time and the benefit of their knowledge. These are people I can always go to with a question. Janet Newcomb, of Newcomb Enterprises; Cordon Bleu pastry chef Karen Stiegler; Janell Percy of Farm Fresh Direct, L.L.C.; Maurice Bratt, of "Dishing with Maurice"; chefs Pierre Pelech and Johannes Bacher; Ted Johnson of AG Accounting, L.L.C.; James Carlberg of Kent SeaTech Corp.; Fred Estrada of L'Artisan Bakery; Jan Boydstun of Kitchen, Kitchen and Pamela Bieri of the California Date Administrative Committee have all been unstinting with answers and advice.

Irena Chalmers, the author of the Julia Child Cookbook Award-winning *The Great Food Almanac* and many other books and instructor of writing at the Culinary Institute of America in Hyde Park, assured me that I could write about food without having a proper culinary training (and my coauthor, Eric Wadlund, more than makes up for my deficits). "Simply report on it, just like you'd report on anything else," she told me sensibly.

I am also grateful to Julie Shirley, who, when she was managing editor of *The Desert Sun* newspaper, first suggested I should write a weekly column about food in the Coachella Valley. No assignment has ever taught me more.

We would both also like to thank Rowena Wadlund and Suzanne Stone for putting up with us!

3

Foreword

WHEN I MOVED TO THE DESERT SEVEN YEARS AGO to redesign and edit a magazine about the Coachella Valley for *The Desert Sun,* the area was obviously in the throes of change. The demographics were shifting enough to make the professional forecasters very busy and extremely happy. A place that had been described as "God's waiting room," perceived as a retirement area for the rich and famous and which traditionally shut down every summer for the four or five hottest months, was turning into a year-round place where there were—gulp!—families, and where the real estate and the hospitality businesses were having to rethink themselves.

In the time since, the change has only intensified. The disparate cities of the valley all have very different personalities and each city has been changing in its own way. Desert Hot Springs, with probably the wildest reputation, a place of natural hot springs, sparsely elegant motels, and even methamphetamine manufacturers going about their business in discreet seclusion, is being developed as one of the still-affordable parts of the desert. At the other end of the valley, Indio, chronologically the first of the cities but for a long time lagging behind more tourist-oriented desert resort towns, has gone into development overdrive, with impressive new country clubs and housing estates.

The food scene has been keeping pace with these changes. At one time, the leading restaurants were either steakhouses or rather formally classic French: Chef Bernard Dervieux's superb Cuistot led the pack, with other pioneers such as Le Vallauris in Palm Springs, its sibling Le St. Germain in Indian Wells, and Wally's Desert Turtle in Rancho Mirage all setting a tone of *comme il faut*. With the turn of the new century a more eclectic and contemporary tone began to be felt. Austrian-born Johannes Bacher opened the eponymous Johannes in Palm Springs, and quickly received national attention from the glossy food magazines. In 2002 James Beard Award–winning chef Jimmy Schmidt brought Rattlesnake Restaurant to the Spotlight 29 Casino in Coachella and set a new standard for the valley's casinos and steakhouses. Then it was the bistro's turn. Pierre Pelech, a veteran from Los Angeles and St. Martin, demonstrated how extraordinary the best classic French bistro food can be with Chez Pierre. Shortly after, Belgian-born Nicolas Klontz and partner Mindy Reed opened Zin, "An American Wine Bistro." That turned out to mean that Klontz could showcase American classics cooked with European scrupulousness while also showing off the wide global range of his background with Spanish, French, Belgian, and Moroccan specials.

Since then, many new restaurants have been springing up by the score across the valley, including such diverse additions to the scene as, in La Quinta, the elegantly Asian Okura and Kevin and Kori Kathman's Blend, which fuses classic and contemporary cuisines. Kathman started his career at the French Laundry in Yountville, and later worked with such luminaries as Gordon Ramsay in London. The background shows.

Since 2003 I have written a weekly food column for *The Desert Sun* (but I do not write restaurant reviews—it's too small a place to be anonymous and I love talking to chefs). In the process I've made good friends—including my coauthor, Chef Eric Wadlund—and had a wonderful time. I have always thought of eating as an adventure and when I first moved here, I was afraid that the adventure might not last. Happily I was wrong.

Henry Fenwick

TABLE OF CONTENTS

CHAPTER *2*: BREAKFAST & BRUNCH   42

TABLE OF CONTENTS

TABLE OF CONTENTS

Table of Contents

TABLE OF CONTENTS

14

LEMON CURD • MOIST LEMON CAKE WITH CREAM CHEESE ICING AND LEMON SORBET • MIRAMONTE SIGNATURE CITRUS DRINK • GRAPEFRUIT, AVOCADO, AND LOBSTER SALAD • GRILLED PORTOBELLO MUSHROOM WITH ARUGULA, PROSCIUTTO DE PARMA, SHAVED PARMIGIANO-REGGIANO, AND WHITE TRUFFLE OIL • SPICY CORN CHOWDER • BABY GREENS • EGGPLANT, TOMATO, AND MOZZARELLA SANDWICH • BEEFSTEAK TOMATOES WITH RICOTTA • MANGO SALSA • MANGO LASSI • SEA SCALLOPS WITH DATE REDUCTION • BRAISED LAMB CHOPS WITH DATES AND NORTH AFRICAN SPICES • KATE'S DATE SHAKE CHEESECAKE • DATE NIB CHOCOLATE CAKE • STICKY DATE PUDDING WITH BUTTERSCOTCH SAUCE • DATE TRUFFLE • DATE AND WALNUT CUSTARD • DATE SHAKE • ESPRESSO-DATE SHAKE

Produce

In the Beginning:
The Banana, the Date and the Orange

THE EARLIEST AMERICANS STARTED IT, seeking peace among the pools, the waterfalls, and the natural hot springs at the foot of the sheltering mountains. Nearly a thousand years ago Native American tribes lived in Palm Springs, cultivating the valleys in the cool weather, finding relief at the higher levels when the heat came. The first European settlers led a life that wasn't too dissimilar from their predecessor's. An 1887 travel poster advertised Palm Springs as *"The home of the Banana, Date and Orange…. Only Spot in California where Frost, Fog and Windstorms are Absolutely Unknown,"* but this was only advertising. The truth was somewhat different.

In fact it was still early days for agriculture in the Coachella Valley. The orange flourished in nearby Redlands and grew well here; the date had been introduced but it was not yet a commercial crop; there may even have been experiments with bananas, but if there were they led nowhere. And the advertisers were definitely much too starry-eyed about the weather. In 1893 a big, 21-day downpour destroyed Palm Springs' irrigation ditches. That catastrophe was immediately followed by an 11-year drought. Many small farmers sold their land and got out.

Fortunately for the valley's future, stronger financial interests were at work. The Southern Pacific Railroad Company was looking for a water source for its steam engines, which stopped at Indio en route to Los Angeles. In 1894 the Rose Well Drilling Company, hired by the railroad, discovered a huge aquifer beneath the Coachella Valley, from Palm Springs to the Salton Sea. That water became an essential part of the development of farmland in the hot, dry desert. The discovery was the birth of the valley as a producer of year-round crops of fruits and vegetables—and the railway carried the produce off to distribute around the country.

It continues to be carried off. The sorrowful little secret of Coachella produce is that though an enormous quantity of the nation's fruits and vegetables are grown here, from grapes to melons, it can be quite hard for a local chef to lay his or her hands on any of it. The farms are large and the produce goes straight to Los Angeles for shipment, much of it abroad. To visit the annual fair in Indio and see the quality of the locally grown citrus, fennel, artichokes, and peppers is a frustrating experience for any local cook. Luckily for residents, grapefruit, lemon, orange, and fig trees flourish in backyards throughout the desert. It's common to see bags of fruit set near the sidewalk with "PLEASE take some" scribbled on a piece of cardboard next to them. Local cooks make good use of that bounty.

The local produce that is readily available throughout the valley is the finally triumphant date. Date palms had in fact been grown in California since Spanish missionaries first planted the seeds around their missions along the coast in the 18th century, but the trees were purely ornamental—the damp coastal climate wasn't good for date production. Date cultivation was not seriously pursued until the U.S. Department of Agriculture imported date palms to the Coachella Valley in 1890. Unfortunately the trees imported were male and, hardly surprisingly, they bore no fruit. (Date farms in the valley typically now grow 50 female trees to one male—a harem-like arrangement that seems to suit the date.)

The California date-growing business only got under way with any efficiency when Deglet Noor offshoots were brought from Algeria in 1900. Several other date varieties, from Egypt and Iraq, began arriving in the years immediately following. Today the Coachella Valley accounts for 95 percent of all the date plantings in the United States (though that is only a small percentage of worldwide date production). The date season lasts, depending on the year's weather patterns, from September through December. An annual Date Festival, with camel races and belly dancers—and dates—is held in February in Indio and has been since 1921. But the date farms of the eastern valley have show rooms and stores where fresh dates can be sampled and bought at their peak of freshness all through harvesttime. Fresh dates are a gourmet treat.

THERE ARE THOUSANDS OF VARIETIES OF DATE, though only a few are grown in the Coachella Valley. There are three categories: soft, semisoft, and dry. The soft has a high moisture content, a comparatively low sugar content, and is both perishable and easily damaged, which makes it difficult to ship. The semisoft has firm flesh, low moisture, and a high sugar content, and is easier to ship. Dry dates are not grown commercially here.

The Deglet Noor, a semisoft date and the first to be grown commercially in the valley, remains the most popular; it's been estimated that the Deglet Noor makes up 80 percent of the dates produced every year (some estimates put it as high as 90 percent). It has a firmer texture than most other dates and is less sweet, which makes it a very good date for cooking, especially for savory dishes.

The Medjool date, plump, soft, and sweet, was brought here in 1927. In a good year, Medjools can be nearly as big as plums and almost as juicy; they are a wonderfully luscious eating date. Their market share is growing; it has been estimated that they account for up to 15 percent of the date harvest in the valley.

AN ARRAY OF OTHER VARIETIES MAKE UP THE REMAINDER of the valley's date crop. Each has its own virtues. It's worth experimenting with different types; sometimes the distinctions are subtle, sometimes very evident. Among the best are the following:

Khadrawy: (Arabic for "green"), first imported from Iraq in 1902. Small, soft, and with a caramel flavor.

Zahidi: another import from Iraq in 1902. It is firm, semisoft, and can be fibrous. It makes a useful alternative to Deglet Noor for cooking.

Halawy: sweet and soft, intensely flavored, with a thin skin. A good eating date.

Honey: a gently flavored, soft date.

Abbada: a California black date with a slightly anisette flavor. It is hard to ship and so can be difficult to find outside the valley.

LEMON CURD

Makes one quart

1 vanilla bean	2½ cups sugar
2 cups fresh lemon juice	2 lemons, zested
16 egg yolks	½ pound butter

In a bowl, combine scraped vanilla bean, lemon juice, zest, sugar, and egg yolks. Whisk together until blended. Pour mixture into a double boiler. Cook over low heat, stirring with a rubber spatula, scraping down the sides. Stir continuously until the curd coats the spatula evenly. Strain mixture if there are lumps. Stir in butter. Chill. Serve.

Courtesy of the Viceroy Hotel

MOIST LEMON CAKE WITH CREAM CHEESE ICING AND LEMON SORBET

Serves six

¾ cup sugar
2 tablespoons unsalted butter
3 egg yolks
1 teaspoon pure vanilla
1 teaspoon lemon zest
2 ounces flour, all-purpose
⅓ cup lemon juice, fresh squeezed
1½ cups buttermilk
3 egg whites
2 tablespoons sugar
2 tablespoons candied lemon
1 pint lemon sorbet

In a tabletop mixer, cream the sugar and butter until just soft. Slowly add the egg yolk, vanilla, and lemon zest, then add the flour and mix until smooth; very slowly add lemon juice and buttermilk. Separately whip the egg whites and sugar until stiff, then gently fold the whipped whites into the lemon batter.

Butter and sugar six, 6-ounce ramekins and pour the batter into the ramekins, dividing evenly among them. Place the ramekins in a water bath and bake in preheated 350°F oven for 60 minutes. Remove the ramekins from the water bath and place them on a cooling rack for 60 minutes.

TO SERVE
Invert the ramekin onto a dessert plate and garnish with the candied lemon, mint leaves, and lemon sorbet.

Courtesy of La Quinta Resort & Club

21

MIRAMONTE SIGNATURE CITRUS DRINK

Serves six

5 Meyer lemons, juice only
2 lemons, juice only
2 blood oranges, segments and zest
2 bottles Orangina, 10 ounces each
6 tops mint
2 cups ice
⅓ cup sugar
1 lemon, sliced thin
1 blood orange, sliced thin

Put all ingredients into a glass pitcher, stir to dissolve sugar, then add the ice and stir.

Courtesy of the Miramonte Resort & Spa

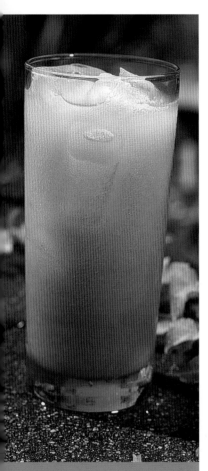

Chef's Tip

By adding some citrus flavored vodka to this recipe you can make an excellent pre-dinner cocktail.

THE MIRAMONTE RESORT & SPA, IN INDIAN WELLS, has orange trees, lemon trees—including six Meyer lemon trees—grapefruit trees, a kumquat, and four large herb beds on the grounds. The Meyer lemon is California's joy; it is thin skinned and less acidic than the regular variety. It has its own distinctive flavor, with a hint of thyme and a touch of mandarin orange, with which it may have been crossed. All the citrus fruit and the mint are handpicked at the Miramonte. The resort garden is a chef's secret weapon.

GRAPEFRUIT, AVOCADO, AND LOBSTER SALAD

Serves four

1 tablespoon olive oil
¼ cup fennel, julienne
¼ cup white wine
6 ounces Maine lobster meat,
  cooked, chilled
2 Coachella sweet grapefruit,
  segments only
1 avocado, cleaned, diced

4 tablespoons Cilantro Mayonnaise,
  recipe below
3 teaspoons lemon juice, fresh
1 teaspoon Tabasco sauce
2 leaves butter lettuce
1 leaf radicchio
Salt and white pepper to taste

Place a large sauté pan over medium heat, add the olive oil and the fennel, sauté until tender and deglaze with white wine, then season with salt and pepper. Remove the fennel from the pan and allow it to cool completely. In a mixing bowl, add the lobster meat, half of the grapefruit, avocado, cilantro mayonnaise, lemon juice, fennel, and Tabasco sauce. Mix well and season with the salt and pepper. Place the butter lettuce and radicchio on a chilled salad plate, then add the grapefruit-lobster salad, and finish by placing the remaining grapefruit segments around the salad.

• •

Cilantro Mayonnaise

3 cups mayonnaise
1 tablespoon lemon juice
½ bunch cilantro, minced
½ teaspoon garlic puree
½ teaspoon cayenne pepper
1 pinch salt

In a mixing bowl, add all of the ingredients and mix together.

Courtesy of Rancho Las Palmas and Chef Leanne Kamekona

Produce

Grilled Portobello Mushroom with Arugula, Prosciutto de Parma, Shaved Parmigiano-Reggiano, and White Truffle Oil

Serves four

The process for this recipe consists of roasting the mushrooms, preparing a vinaigrette dressing, then assembling the ingredients into the final dish.

4 portobello mushrooms, large, roasted, recipe below
½ cup arugula or baby arugula (locally grown)
2 ounces Prosciutto de Parma, sliced very thin
¼ cup shaved Parmigiano-Reggiano curls (use a vegetable peeler)
¼ cup Balsamic Vinaigrette, recipe follows
¼ cup extra-virgin olive oil to brush on the mushrooms
1 tablespoon white truffle oil to drizzle on plate
Salt and pepper to taste

Roasted Portobello Mushrooms

Brush the cleaned mushrooms with olive oil and season with salt and pepper. Place the mushrooms on a small sheet pan and baked at 400°F for approximately 10 minutes, until the mushrooms start to sweat. Remove from oven and cool.

Chef's Tip

Remove the stems and dark "gills" from under the mushroom cap before cooking. The gills can be removed gently with a tablespoon. This will help to keep the portobello a nice light brown color and prevent it from turning black.

24

Balsamic Vinaigrette

2 tablespoons aged balsamic vinegar, 18-year-old vintage
½ cup extra-virgin olive oil, a blend of Arbequena and Moroccan
1 shallot, minced
1 garlic clove, minced
Salt and pepper to taste

In a mixing bowl combine all ingredients and whisk together.

To Finish

With a sharp knife or serrated knife slice the mushroom into 5 pieces at a 45-degree angle and fan the pieces onto a plate, then place the prosciutto on the mushroom. Toss the arugula with the balsamic vinaigrette and adjust seasoning with salt and pepper if needed. Place the arugula salad on top of the prosciutto and mushroom. Garnish with shaved Parmigiano-Reggiano curls and drizzle with white truffle oil.

Courtesy of the Miramonte Resort & Spa and Chef Sarah Bowman

25

SPICY CORN CHOWDER

Serves six

¼ pound bacon, cooked, drained, and crumbled, reserving the bacon grease
1 tablespoon butter, unsalted
1 cup finely diced onion
1 cup finely diced celery
1 cup finely diced carrots
¼ cup flour
3 cups corn, freshly cut from the cob
½ cup chicken stock
1 bay leaf
1 teaspoon thyme
1½ cups potatoes
2 finely diced roma tomatoes
4 jalapeños, minced
Salt and pepper to taste

Put a heavy-duty sauce pan over medium-high heat; add the butter and bacon grease. When it is warm, add the onion, celery, and carrot and sauté until translucent, do not brown. Season with salt and pepper. Sprinkle with flour and stir to "cook" the flour. Next add the chicken stock, corn, bay leaf, thyme, and potatoes, and bring to a boil. Lower the heat and simmer for 45 to 55 minutes.

While the chowder is simmering, make the salsa by mixing the tomatoes and jalapeños, then seasoning with salt and pepper. Serve the chowder in warm bowls and garnish with the crumbled bacon and fiery salsa.

Courtesy of Jillian's Restaurant, Chef Jay Trubee

Chef's Tip

Adding the flour will form the roux that will thicken the soup. It is important to cook this shortening-flour mixture for 3 to 5 minutes, but do not brown. By cooking the roux you will have a richer-tasting corn chowder.

BABY GREENS

Serves four

4 chilled plates
1 bag baby greens
1 fennel bulb
¼ cup almonds
1 cup haricot vert or green beans

¼ cup feta cheese
¼ cup Lemon-Herb Vinaigrette,
  recipe below
Salt and pepper to taste

Lemon-Herb Vinaigrette

3 garlic cloves
6 lemons, juice only
1 shallot
1 teaspoon Dijon mustard
Salt and pepper to taste
2 tablespoons honey

¾ cup grapeseed or canola oil
1 cup olive oil
¼ bunch parsley
¼ bunch tarragon
¼ bunch chervil

In a blender, add garlic, juice from lemons, shallot, Dijon mustard, salt and pepper. Blend until smooth. Add honey. Blend again. While blender is running, slowly add oils until "creamy" consistency. Chop the herbs and stir in.

TO FINISH
Shave the fennel bulb on a mandoline, toss with olive oil, salt and pepper to taste. Lay the fennel out on a jellyroll pan and roast at 350°F for 10 minutes or until golden brown. Cool, set aside. Blanch the green beans; shock in an ice bath to stop cooking. Pat the green beans dry. In a large bowl, add baby greens, roasted fennel, almonds, and green beans. Add vinaigrette, just enough to dress the salad, and place on the chilled plates. Garnish with feta cheese, cut into cubes, 3 per salad.

Courtesy of the Viceroy Hotel

Chef's Tip

A mandoline is a French handheld slicer, used in industrial kitchens. For home use, the Japanese version is smaller and easier to use.

Produce

JANELL PERCY DOES NOT NEED TO WORRY about where to find local produce. An agronomist who heads up a consulting company, Farm Fresh Direct, Janell is active in the Coachella Valley branch of California Women for Agriculture, is a driving force in the valley 4-H Club the Desert Sandblasters (her sons are frequently prize-winning members), and grows a lot of her own fruit and vegetables. She has a regular spot, Agmoment, on the valley television food show *Chow Hound*, on TV10. Her Eggplant, Tomato and Mozzarella Sandwich recipe follows.

EGGPLANT, TOMATO, AND MOZZARELLA SANDWICH

Serves four

2 eggplants
1 egg, beaten
¼ cup parmesan cheese, grated
2 baguettes, crisp
½ cup mayonnaise, flavored with fresh chopped thyme
2 heirloom tomatoes, sliced
2 slices Mozzarella cheese
4 sprigs thyme, fresh, chopped
Sea salt and freshly ground black pepper to taste

Slice eggplants lengthwise into thin pieces, brush with the egg, sprinkle with parmesan cheese, and broil on each side. Split baguette and layer with mayonnaise to taste, broiled eggplant, tomatoes, and cheese and sprinkle with thyme. Season and close baguette. Cut into pieces and serve.

Courtesy of Janell Percy

BEEFSTEAK TOMATOES WITH RICOTTA

Serves four

2 beefsteak tomatoes, red, large, diced
1 beefsteak tomato, orange, large, diced
1 beefsteak tomato, yellow, large, diced
⅛ cup tarragon, fresh, chopped
½ cup ricotta cheese
2 tablespoons extra-virgin olive oil
1 tablespoon red chili oil
Sea salt and black pepper to taste

In a large mixing bowl add the tomatoes, tarragon, and half of the olive oil and season with salt and black pepper. Place 3 rounds of the ricotta on each salad plate and then divide the tomatoes among the plates. Drizzle the tomatoes with remaining olive oil and the chili oil.

Courtesy of Chef Eric Wadlund, Beefsteak Restaurant

LUCKILY FOR VALLEY COOKS, THERE ARE A FEW LOCAL FARMS whose produce is not completely dedicated to the major purveyors. Freshly picked fruit and vegetables can be found in the east valley by those who are determined enough: strawberries, tomatoes, lettuces, and corn can all be bought in season—though the Coachella Valley season is not quite the same as elsewhere. Tomatoes and strawberries are out of season by July, and valley corn is harvested in September. Though there is no longer a certified farmer's market in the valley, a fruit and vegetable stand at the corner of Madison and Highway 111 sells produce directly from the nearby fields during the growing season.

Chef's Tip

The tomatoes are the center of this salad, so for the best results buy heirloom beefsteak tomatoes.

Produce

MANGOES WERE INTRODUCED TO THE UNITED STATES in Florida, however Hurricane Andrew had destroyed the commercial mango farms there. As a result, the Coachella Valley has the largest area of commercially grown mangoes in North America, many of them organic. This fact remains widely unknown; even in the valley not many realize that great mangoes grow here. The producers have experimented with a range of varieties but the one they now grow is the Keitt, a green-skinned mango with a nonfibrous texture and a wonderful flavor. Slowly, American consumers are beginning to understand that red mangoes are not necessarily the best; in fact they are probably not nearly as good as the green. Keitt mangoes hold on the trees longer than other varieties and valley mangoes are harvested in September, after the Mexican crop has finished. If you are lucky enough to find local mangoes, grab as many as you can.

MANGO SALSA *Makes two cups*

1 mango, peeled, diced medium
½ jalapeño pepper, diced fine
¼ red onion, diced fine
1 lime, juice only
2 tablespoons extra-virgin olive oil

1 tablespoon cilantro, chopped fine
½ red pepper, diced fine
Sea salt and freshly ground
   red pepper to taste

Place all ingredients in a mixing bowl and mix well; season with salt and pepper.

Courtesy of Janell Percy

MANGO LASSI *Serves six*

1 mango, ripe
1 cup plain yogurt
1 cup milk

1 teaspoon sugar, or to taste
1 pinch saffron
1 cup ice

Chop the mango into small pieces and blend in an electric blender; depending on the size of the mango this should produce about half a cup of mango pulp. Add the yogurt and blend. Mix the milk with sugar to taste, then blend into the mango mixture. Stir in the pinch of saffron. Serve over ice cubes or crushed ice in a tall glass.

Courtesy of Henry Fenwick

Chef's Tip

If fresh mangoes are unavailable, Indian grocery stores often stock canned mango pulp; these are most likely to be Alphonso mangoes, which are popular in India. This recipe is based on one given to me by Chef Roy Chowdhary; he also adds ¼ teaspoon of green cardamom powder along with the saffron.

SEA SCALLOPS WITH DATE REDUCTION

Serves four

This recipe uses a date reduction and a vin blanc sauce to dress up the sea scallops.

16 sea scallops, extra-large
2 teaspoons canola oil
2 cups Israeli couscous, cooked
1 lemon, zest and segments
1 bunch green onion, white part only, minced
6 dates, skinned, pitted, and diced
¼ cup Date Paste, recipe below
1 cup Vin Blanc, recipe follows
½ cup butter, unsalted, cubed
2 teaspoons water
1 tablespoon cilantro, chopped
Sea salt and white pepper to taste

Date Paste

2 cups dates, skinned, pitted, and diced
6 cups white wine

Blend the dates and wine until smooth, strain through a fine strainer. Place a thick-bottomed saucepan over medium-low heat and add the date-wine mixture. Reduce slowly until it becomes very thick; remove from heat and let cool.

Continued on next page

Chef's Tip

You can use any date for this recipe but I use a locally grown date called Deglet Noor. Give them a try, as they have a great flavor that is not too sweet.

31

Vin Blanc

1 bottle white wine
¼ cup shallot, sliced
2 bay leaves
2 tablespoons thyme
3 quarts heavy cream
Sea salt and white pepper to taste

In a medium stockpot sweat the shallots. Deglaze with white wine and reduce. Add the bay leaves and thyme, and reduce the white wine mixture to about 2 cups. Add heavy cream and reduce approximately by half; strain through a fine strainer. Season to taste, and reserve for use.

To Finish
Place a small saucepan over medium-high heat and add the water; bring to a boil. Whip in the butter a couple of cubes at a time, add the date paste, season with salt and white pepper, and set aside, keeping warm. Place a small saucepan over medium heat and add the couscous, lemon, green onion, and vin blanc, stirring the whole time, then finish by adding the dates, salt, and white pepper. Set aside and keep warm. Season the scallops with salt and white pepper. Place a large sauté pan over a medium-high heat, add the canola oil, and then sear the scallops, cooking until medium.

To Serve
Place about ½ cup of the couscous mixture in the middle of the plate and then top with 4 seared scallops. Spoon the date paste around the plate and then garnish with the chopped cilantro.

Courtesy of Chef Eric Wadlund, Beefsteak Restaurant

DATES ARE HONORED MORE IN THE MIDDLE EAST than they are here in the United States. The California Date Administrative Committee (CDAC) and the California Date Commission have been hard at work together, trying to get the California date some respect, especially in its home state. An amateur date recipe contest is held every year at the National Date Festival, with winners in five categories: bread, entrée, salad, dessert and confection. In April there is a Professional Chef competition, sponsored by the CDAC, that draws entries from all over the country. There are prizes for best appetizer, best entrée and best dessert, plus Best of Show and People's Choice awards. Audrey Pitruzella is a regular contestant in the amateur date recipe contest. The following recipe was a winner in the entrée category. It's not only good, it's easy to make.

BRAISED LAMB CHOPS WITH DATES AND NORTH AFRICAN SPICES

Serves four

4 lamb shoulder chops, ¾ inch thick and trimmed of external fat	½ teaspoon ground cinnamon
2 tablespoons olive oil	⅛ teaspoon cayenne pepper
1 small onion	1 cup tomatoes, in puree, canned
2 cloves garlic, minced	2 tablespoons honey
1 teaspoon ground coriander	1 cup dates, whole, without pits
½ teaspoon ground cumin	3 tablespoons cilantro, chopped
	Salt and pepper to taste

Sprinkle chops with salt and pepper. Heat 1 tablespoon of oil in large heavy-bottomed skillet over medium-high heat. Add lamb chops and brown on both sides, 4–5 minutes. Remove chops from pan and set aside. Pour excess fat from pan, return to medium-high heat, and add remaining olive oil, onion, and garlic. Add spices; cook until fragrant, about 1 minute. Stir in tomatoes with puree and honey, scraping up browned bits from pan. Return chops to pan; cover and cook on low heat until tender, 15–20 minutes. Stir in dates and cilantro before serving.

Courtesy of Audrey Pitruzella and the California Date Administrative Committee

Chef's Tip

This dish goes very well with saffron-flavored couscous.

KATIE CATHCART WON IN THE DESSERT CATEGORY at the amateur recipe contest while she was beginning her undergraduate work at UCLA. Her Date Shake Cheesecake recipe follows.

KATE'S DATE SHAKE CHEESECAKE

Makes one cake

This cheesecake consists of a crust, cheesecake with filling, and a topping.

. . . .

Crust

½ cup chopped pecans
½ cup date crystals
1¼ cup graham cracker crumbs
¼ cup sugar
6 tablespoons melted margarine

Preheat oven to 350°F. Crush chopped pecans into a fine crumble. Mix together with rest of crust ingredients. Spread mixture evenly into the base of a greased 9-inch spring-form pan and cook for 8 minutes. Remove from the oven and let cool.

Chef's Tip

The trick to having a moist cheesecake is to underbake it; the middle of the cake should be slightly loose when you remove it from the oven. Note: date sugar and date crystals are made from dehydrated dates. One cup of date crystals plus ⅓ cup of liquid is the equivalent of one cup of chopped dates. Date sugar (ground finer than the crystals) can be substituted for white sugar when cooking, though liquid may need to be added.

Filling

2½ cups pitted, chopped Deglet Noor dates
1 cup water
¼ cup sugar
1 teaspoon vanilla

In a saucepan, combine the chopped dates, water, and sugar. Stir constantly over medium-high heat until just before the mixture begins to boil, about 2 minutes. Reduce temperature to low and continue to thicken the mixture until all date pieces are tender, about 5 minutes. Quickly pour into a blender and add vanilla. Mix on high to break apart bigger pieces, about 4 minutes. Spoon the filling onto the crust.

Cheesecake

4 cups cream cheese (4 packages)
4 eggs
1 cup sugar
1 teaspoon vanilla

In a mixer at medium speed, combine the cream cheese, sugars and vanilla. Add the eggs and continue to mix until well blended. Pour over filling and bake in a preheated 350°F oven for 50 minutes; remove from the oven and let cool.

Topping

1 cup dextrose-coated diced dates   **½ cup spreadable caramel topping**
1 teaspoon powdered sugar

Process diced dates in a blender until a crumble forms. Remove and mix in powdered sugar to break up pieces. Scatter dates on top of cheesecake and drizzle with caramel topping. Refrigerate for 4 hours or overnight.

Courtesy of Katie Cathcart and the California Date Administrative Committee

DATE NIB CHOCOLATE CAKE

Serves twelve

1¼ pounds butter, unsalted
1½ pounds semisweet chocolate
½ cup flour
9 egg yolks
9 eggs
2 cups granulated sugar
⅓ cup cocoa nibs (small crushed pieces of cocoa)
2 cups Halaway dates, chopped
2 cups Chocolate Mirror Glaze, recipe below

Melt the butter with the chocolate over a water bath. When melted, set aside. In a mixing bowl blend the eggs and egg yolks together, then slowly incorporate the sugar and the flour. Add the chocolate mixture and the finely chopped dates. Slowly fold in the cocoa nibs. Bake in 2-inch pastry metal rings or mini muffin mold at 330°F for 10–12 minutes. Remove from oven and let rest an hour before removing from the mold. To serve, cover the cake with the chocolate mirror glaze.

Chocolate Mirror Glaze

1 gelatin sheet
Scant ½ cup corn syrup
2 cups heavy cream
1½ cups semisweet dark chocolate

Soak the gelatin sheet in cold water. In a saucepan mix the corn syrup and the heavy cream and bring to a boil. Add the chocolate and the gelatin sheet (without any excess of water).

Courtesy of Chef Jerome Diop, Renaissance Esmeralda Resort & Spa

STICKY DATE PUDDING
WITH BUTTERSCOTCH SAUCE

6 cups dates, chopped
6 cups water
4 teaspoons baking soda
1 pound butter
3 cups sugar
8 eggs
5 cups flour
Butterscotch Sauce, recipe below

Heat dates and water slowly, then add baking soda. Cool. Beat together butter, sugar, and eggs. Fold this mixture into the dates and flour. Bake in water bath at 375°F for 1½ hours, adding butterscotch sauce 10 minutes before pudding has finished cooking.

Butterscotch Sauce

2 cups brown sugar
2 cups cream
1 pound butter, unsalted
2 teaspoons pure vanilla extract

Combine sugar, cream, and butter and heat slowly. Add vanilla to taste.

Courtesy of Chef Jay Trubee, Jillian's Restaurant

 *Produce*

DATE TRUFFLE

Makes twelve

1 cup heavy cream
1 pound dark chocolate
1 cup Zahidi dates, pureed
2 tablespoons Myers dark rum
¼ cup cocoa or powdered dark chocolate

Boil the heavy cream and add the chocolate and the date puree. Then stir in the rum. Refrigerate overnight. With a small ice-cream scoop form small balls of mixture and, using your hands (wearing plastic gloves), roll them over dark chocolate powder or cocoa two times.

Courtesy of Chef Jerome Diop, Renaissance Esmeralda Resort & Spa

DATE AND WALNUT CUSTARD

Serves eight

¼ cup cornstarch
1 quart half-and-half
4 egg yolks
1 cup sugar
⅓ cup dates, chopped
4 dates, halved, for garnish
¼ cup walnuts, chopped
8 walnut halves for garnish
1 orange, zest only

Dissolve cornstarch in 1 cup half-and-half, stirring well. Pour remainder of half-and-half into a saucepan, place over medium heat, then add orange zest and simmer slowly. Beat the egg yolks together until creamy, then add to the mixture, stirring frequently. Add cornstarch mixture and keep stirring. Add chopped dates and walnuts and simmer gently for 5 minutes. Remove from heat and then divide into 8 ramekins. Garnish each serving with a date half and a walnut half and refrigerate. Serve chilled.

Courtesy of Henry Fenwick

Produce

"IF DATES AND MILK MAKE THE PERFECT FOOD,
THE DATE SHAKE IS A GIFT FROM HEAVEN."

—Jeffrey Steingarten

DATE SHAKES HAVE BEEN SERVED TO TRAVELERS, tourists, and residents ever since dates were harvested here— who created the first one is lost in history. They have become a desert icon; those who are Palm Springs bound from Los Angeles will find date shakes advertised at Hadley's, just off of Highway 10, shortly before they come to the Palm Springs exit. Those heading east along Highway 111 through Indio can't miss Shields Date Farm, which advertises its date shakes prominently, along with a film that promises to reveal all about the sex life of the date. The shakes are filling, delicious, full of calories, and give enough energy to make anyone feel ready for anything. It's the ideal traveler's fast food. And in smaller servings it makes a great end to a meal.

DATE SHAKE

1 cup pitted, coarsely chopped dates
1 quart whole milk
2 pints French vanilla ice cream
1 teaspoon grated fresh nutmeg

For each date shake, place ¼ cup dates in a blender. Add 1 cup cold whole milk and 2 big scoops of French vanilla ice cream. Add grated nutmeg into blender. Blend until smooth.

Courtesy of Chef Eric Wadlund, Beefsteak Restaurant

ESPRESSO-DATE SHAKE

1 cup pitted, coarsely chopped dates
1 quart whole milk
1 pint French vanilla ice cream
1 pint coffee ice cream
1 teaspoon decaffeinated espresso

For each date shake, place ¼ cup dates in a blender. Add 1 cup cold milk, 1 big scoop of French vanilla ice cream, and 1 big scoop of coffee ice cream, followed by ¼ teaspoon of fresh espresso. Blend until smooth.

Courtesy of Chef Eric Wadlund, Beefsteak Restaurant

ORIGINAL JOE'S EGGS • BREAKFAST BURRITO • YOGURT-GRANOLA PARFAIT • LOBSTER BENEDICT • HAM AND BRIE CREPES • NORMA'S EGGS BENEDICT • BUTTERMILK PANCAKES WITH MACADAMIA NUT AND BANANA COMPOTE • BLUEBERRY-LEMON MUFFINS • GRAPEFRUIT, GINGER, AND RUM MARMALADE

Breaking Your Fast

ONE OF PALM SPRINGS' SADDEST SIGHTS MUST BE THAT OF A GROUP of visiting out-of-towners, obviously just out of bed and desperate for a decent cup of coffee, searching for a breakfast better than the one provided at their motel. Luckily there are places for them to go—after all, even residents like to go out for breakfast, so the demand is constant. In a place where people are apt to be out on the golf course at six in the morning (a pleasantly cool time of day for a round), brunch is a natural segue after a game.

One of the valley's oldest and best-loved havens, Louise's Pantry, first opened in 1946, called after its owner, Louise Leavelle. The original Pantry was housed in a downtown Palm Springs drugstore. It soon became a local institution and, needing more space, it changed location. Next door to the Plaza Theatre (the Palm Springs movie house, where Garbo had sometimes visited for premieres and where the renowned Palm Springs Follies now has its home), the café was so popular that there were lines outside from the moment they opened until the time they closed. The queues for the movies and the queues for the café sometimes got mixed up.

The restaurant has moved and changed hands several times since then; for a brief period there were three branches in the valley. Now the one remaining—and the newest—Pantry is thriving in La Quinta. They still have some of the same accessories from their old Palm Springs establishment, and, more importantly, some of the veteran staff and much of the same menu. They still serve breakfast all day.

ORIGINAL JOE'S EGGS

Serves four

8 eggs, whipped
½ cup cooked and chopped spinach
½ cup cooked and chopped mushrooms
½ cup cooked ground beef
2 tablespoons canola oil
Salt and black pepper to taste

Place a 12-inch nonstick skillet over medium-high heat, add the oil then the eggs, and season with the salt and pepper. Cook until medium done, then add the mushrooms, spinach, and beef. Continue cooking until desired doneness.

Courtesy of Louise's Pantry

BREAKFAST BURRITO

Serves four

8 eggs, whipped
½ cup chopped and cooked onions
½ cup cooked and diced green chiles
⅓ cup Monterey Jack cheese
½ cup cheddar cheese
2 tablespoons canola oil
4 flour tortillas, 12-inch
1 cup salsa, spicy
½ cup sour cream
Salt and black pepper to taste

Place a 12-inch nonstick skillet over medium-high heat, add the oil then the eggs, and season with the salt and pepper. Cook until medium done, then add the onions and chiles. Continue cooking until desired doneness. Warm the four tortillas, then lay them out flat. Spread the egg and chile mixture on the tortillas and top with the cheeses. Fold in the sides and roll up to form the burritos. Cut in half and serve with salsa and sour cream.

Courtesy of Louise's Pantry

YOGURT-GRANOLA PARFAIT

Serves four

2 cups granola
1 quart yogurt, plain
1 pint sliced strawberries
1 pint sliced raspberries
2 bananas, sliced

In 4 tall parfait glasses, layer the granola, yogurt, and fruit.
Repeat 2 or 3 times to fill glass. Decorate with berries.

Courtesy of More Than a Mouthful Catering

LOBSTER BENEDICT

Serves four

4 English muffins
4 cups fresh spinach, sautéed
2 roma tomatoes, diced
½ pound lobster meat, cooked
8 large eggs
1 cup hollandaise sauce, see recipe on page 51

Poach all the eggs in water until cooked medium-rare. Toast the English muffins until golden brown. Place two muffins side by side on each plate; place the sautéed spinach on top of the muffins. Next place the lobster meat on the spinach, then the poached eggs. Finish by topping with hollandaise sauce.

Courtesy of More Than a Mouthful Catering

MANY OF THE AREA'S RESORTS HAVE MADE WEEKEND BRUNCH a popular feature, appealing to locals as well as to visitors. The boutique hotels in particular have become good breakfast destinations. At Parker Palm Springs, their all-day restaurant, Norma's, attracts folk from Palm Springs as well as guests from Los Angeles and the East Coast. There is a formidable array of Benedict recipes on their breakfast menu and many of their breakfast dishes are served all day, for those who march to a different schedule.

HAM AND BRIE CREPES

Serves one

**2 crepes, 8 to 10 inches
    (recipe below)
3 slices Black Forest ham, thinly sliced**

**3 pieces Brie
1 cup home-fried potatoes
Mache lettuce**

Crepes

**¾ cup flour
3 eggs
3 egg yolks**

**⅓ cup butter, melted
1½ cups warm milk
1 pinch salt**

In a mixing bowl add the flour, eggs and egg yolks, mix slightly, then add the melted butter, warm milk, and cinnamon and mix well. Season with salt.

TO FINISH
Place 2 crepes on a plate side by side, overlapping by 2 inches, then place 3 thin slices of ham on the crepes and top with 3 pieces of Brie side by side. Place in 350°F oven for 2–3 minutes to allow the cheese to melt and warm the ham. Remove the ham melt from the oven and allow to cool only slightly. Roll crepes into tube shape and cut on bias twice to equal 3 pieces. To serve, place home fries in the center of a plate and place the 3 pieces of ham and brie crepes over the potatoes, slightly standing up, equally spaced on the plate. Garnish with mache lettuce and serve.

Courtesy of Parker Palm Springs

Chef's Tip

For buckwheat crepes, replace ⅓ cup regular flour with ⅓ cup of buckwheat flour.

49

NORMA'S EGGS BENEDICT

Serves four

This recipe requires the preparation of pancakes and hollandaise sauce.

8 eggs, large
1 quart water
1 tablespoon vinegar
8 slices Canadian bacon
16 asparagus spears, blanched
8 Pancakes, small, recipe below
1 cup Hollandaise Sauce, recipe follows
½ cup mache lettuce

Place a large saucepot over medium-high heat and add water and vinegar. Bring to a boil, then reduce the heat to a simmer and add the eggs. Poach the eggs until soft. Place the two pancakes on the plate; top with the Canadian bacon, asparagus, and eggs and then the sauce; garnish with mache lettuce.

. . . .

Pancakes

1 cup buttermilk
10 tablespoons melted butter
½ cup plus 2 tablespoons milk
4¼ cups flour
4½ cups sugar

6 eggs
1½ tablespoons baking powder
1 tablespoon baking soda
1 orange, zest only
1 pinch salt

In a mixing bowl combine all of the wet ingredients and the orange zest. Be sure to whisk the ingredients well to mix the eggs and the buttermilk. In another large mixing bowl, combine all the dry ingredients and mix well. Add the wet ingredients to the dry ingredients, and fold with a spatula until blended. Add melted butter, and continue to stir with spatula until mixture is well incorporated and some lumps are still in the batter. Ladle batter onto non-stick or lightly buttered skillet or griddle, brown and flip.

Hollandaise Sauce

3 egg yolks
3 tablespoons hot water
¾ cup clarified butter, warm
½ lemon, juice only
Salt and pepper to taste

Place a large saucepan over medium-high heat and add about ½ inch water. Place the egg yolks and the 3 tablespoons hot water in a large mixing bowl. Whisk the yolks and water until light and frothy, then place the bowl over, but not in, the simmering water. Whip until the egg mixture thickens, 3–5 minutes. Reduce the heat to low and slowly add the clarified butter a little at a time while whisking continuously. Remove from the heat and finish by whipping in the lemon juice. Season with salt and pepper.

Courtesy of Parker Palm Springs

UNTIL PARKER PALM SPRINGS OPENED, the Viceroy Hotel had the clear title of hippest small hotel in Palm Springs. Now they vie for the position, though the rather larger Parker's has drawn the most publicity. The restaurant and bar at the Viceroy, Citron, is small, mirrored, and summery, and its brunch is a featured attraction for locals.

BUTTERMILK PANCAKES WITH MACADAMIA NUT AND BANANA COMPOTE

Serves four

1 cup flour	1 cup buttermilk, well shaken
1 teaspoon baking soda	Macadamia Nut and Banana
½ teaspoon salt	Compote, recipe below
1 large egg	

In a large mixing bowl, whisk all dry ingredients together, then whisk in eggs and buttermilk. Blend well but still leaving some lumps. Ladle batter onto non-stick or lightly buttered skillet or griddle, brown and flip.

Macadamia Nut and Banana Compote

1½ cup macadamia nuts, raw	2½ cups maple syrup
1 tablespoon butter, unsalted	2 bananas
1 vanilla bean, scraped	

Sauté the macadamia nuts in butter until they begin to turn light brown, then add the maple syrup and scraped vanilla bean; you may add in the vanilla bean skin to maximize flavor. Simmer until syrup reduces to a saucelike consistency. Chop bananas, then add them into the macadamia nut syrup just before serving.

Courtesy of Citron Restaurant, the Viceroy Hotel

FOR DIEHARD COOKS (and we assume that anyone reading this book is probably to be counted in that category), giving a brunch party at home is one of the best ways to celebrate living in the desert. We have gathered the following recipes from desert residents who think that way.

BLUEBERRY-LEMON MUFFINS

2 cups flour
⅓ cup sugar
3 teaspoons baking powder
1 teaspoon salt
¾ cup milk
2 tablespoons melted butter
⅓ cup vegetable oil
1 egg
1 lemon, zest only
1 cup fresh blueberries
1 pinch raw or turbinado sugar

Preheat oven to 400°F. Line a 12-muffin tin with paper baking cups, or grease bottoms of muffin cups. In medium bowl whisk together flour, sugar, baking powder, and salt. In large bowl whisk together milk, butter, oil, egg, and lemon zest. Pour dry ingredients, all at once, into wet ingredients, and stir together until dry ingredients are just moistened (batter will be lumpy). Do not overmix! Fold in blueberries gently. Spoon batter evenly into muffin cups. Sprinkle with raw sugar. Bake until golden brown, 18–20 minutes. Immediately remove muffins from pan to cooling rack.

Courtesy of Pastry Chef Karen Stiegler

Chef's Tip

These muffins are a perfect treat for breakfast, brunch, or even an afternoon snack. The butter gives richness without a heavy crumb, and the oil and baking powder keep the muffins light. One egg in the recipe makes a true muffin and not a cupcake, while the blueberries serve up your antioxidants. The raw sugar baked on top adds a nice crunch!

GRAPEFRUIT, GINGER, AND RUM MARMALADE

Makes four 8-ounce jars

1¾ pounds grapefruit (2–3 fruits)
5 cups sugar
2 lemons, juice only
1 ginger root, 2-inch piece, fresh, peeled, and minced
¼ cup dark rum

Place the grapefruit in a large saucepan and fill with enough water to ensure that the fruit floats freely. Bring to a boil and simmer for about 2 hours, adding hot water if liquid boils away. Drain. Slice the cooked grapefruit thinly, then chop, using the whole fruit, pith and all. Remove seeds. Put grapefruit back in saucepan and add sugar, lemon juice, and ginger root. Let sugar dissolve over gentle heat, then bring to boil, add half the rum and simmer for 15 minutes. Cool slightly. Stir in the rest of the rum. Ladle into sterilized jars and close the lids. Keeps 4–6 months in refrigerator.

Courtesy of Henry Fenwick

Skewered Striped Bass with Ponzu Dipping Sauce • Salomon's Ceviche • Honey-Soy Glazed Sea Bass • Sugar-Spiced Salmon • Roasted Alaskan Halibut • Seared Hawaiian Ahi • Lobster Tacos • John Dory with Brioche and Tomatoes • Dover Sole with Lemon Sauce • Hamachi Carpaccio with Soy-Lemon Vinaigrette

The Unexpected Crop: Fish in the Desert

THE VALLEY IS KNOWN FOR ITS VEGETABLES AND FRUIT, but one major local farm product is less advertised: fish. There are several small fish farms in the desert, raising tilapia and trout, but the largest fish farm in the valley also happens to be the largest hybrid striped bass farm in the world. Kent SeaTech, in Mecca, ships 80,000 pounds of California-farmed striped bass every week from its 160-acre facility. The bass they raise is a cross between the Atlantic striped bass and the freshwater striped bass— fast growing, robust, and meaty.

The fish aren't born in the valley; they're shipped in as fingerlings from Arkansas by the truckload. Some go into cold-water tanks to slow their growth and ensure that there is a continual year-round supply of maturing fish. In the warm-water tanks the rest mature quickly; they're fed manually so that their progress can be tracked.

Kent SeaTech has been in the Coachella Valley now for over 20 years and they have developed a close working relationship with the surrounding farms; the water they use is recycled several times, then made available to farmers and neighboring duck-hunting clubs. Good water sharing makes for good neighbors.

A MAJOR SHIFT IS CURRENTLY TAKING PLACE in the Coachella Valley. The old demographics are changing, among both residents and visitors. The average age of the population is dropping and visitors are increasingly well traveled. More and more people live in the area year-round, and expectations for the quantity and quality of fish are higher than even five years ago. This has meant a pronounced rise in the service the valley gets from purveyors; when once supplies of fish would arrive from the coast weekly, now they arrive daily. Just as important has been the rise of faster shipping methods. Overnight shipping has revolutionized the restaurant business. A chef in the desert today can come into his or her office at 9 a.m, call the docks in Hawaii, find out what catch is best that morning, place an order in time to catch that day's shipment from the islands, and have the fish in the kitchen the following morning, 24 hours after it was caught.

SKEWERED STRIPED BASS WITH PONZU DIPPING SAUCE

Serves six

6 striped bass filets, skinless
¼ cup olive oil
Sea salt and freshly ground white pepper to taste
1 cup Ponzu Dipping Sauce, recipe below

Cut filets lengthwise into 1½-inch strips. Thread strips onto skewers and brush with olive oil, then sprinkle with salt and pepper. Place half the skewers over a hot grill fire and grill for 3 minutes per side. Lay on half sheet pan in a warming oven to keep warm. Serve warm with Ponzu dipping sauce.

Chef's Tip

Finished skewers should be removed from the warming oven and then served within 10 minutes.

Ponzu Dipping Sauce

½ cup soy sauce, low sodium
¼ cup rice wine vinegar

½ cup orange juice
1 tablespoon sugar

In a mixing bowl blend all ingredients well.

Courtesy of Kent SeaTech Corporation

MAGDALENO SALOMON IS A FISH CULTURIST at Kent SeaTech Corporation in Mecca, California. He gave us his own recipe for ceviche, using the fish he farms. It's a popular recipe among his coworkers and he always makes a large amount.

SALOMON'S CEVICHE

Serves 25 to 35

Plan ahead for this crowd recipe, as it requires overnight marinating.

8 pounds California-farmed striped bass, boneless filets, diced
1½ quarts lime juice

In a large container combine the bass and lime juice; mix thoroughly and then let cure overnight in the refrigerator. The lime juice "cooks" the fish. In the morning drain most of the excess lemon juice and combine with:

2 pounds white onions, diced fine
4 cucumbers, peeled and diced
2 bunches cilantro, chopped medium fine
1 bunch celery, diced
½ pound garlic, fresh, peeled, smashed, and chopped fine
½ pound jalapeños diced with seeds (increase for more heat)
5 pounds tomatoes, diced
1 pint ketchup
1½ pints Clamato juice
3 Hass avocados, diced

Mix gently until all ingredients are combined. Serve with fried whole corn tortillas or corn tortilla chips.

Courtesy of Magdaleno Salomon

Honey-Soy Glazed Sea Bass

Serves four

4 sea bass filets, 7 ounces each
2 tablespoons olive oil
Salt and pepper to taste
½ cup Honey-Soy Glaze, recipe follows
¾ cup Green Curry Coconut Paste, recipe follows

Heat a large sauté pan over high heat, season fish with salt and pepper. Place fish in the hot pan and cook till golden brown on one side, about 3 minutes, then turn over and finish cooking in a preheated 350°F oven for about 5 minutes. Remove from oven. Turn oven to broil. Turn fish back over to golden browned side and coat with a tablespoon of the reserved honey-soy glaze; flash under the broiler to finish. Serve with steamed rice, baby bok choy and green curry coconut sauce.

Chef's Tip

This is an excellent green curry paste recipe. You will have a lot left over, so put it in an airtight container and keep it refrigerated. It goes very well with shrimp and pork.

Honey-Soy Glaze

2 tablespoons honey
2 tablespoons brown sugar
2 tablespoons soy sauce

In a small bowl, whisk the ingredients together till the sugar is dissolved, and reserve.

. . . .

Green Curry Coconut Paste

6 tablespoons fresh ginger, chopped fine
6 cloves fresh garlic, chopped fine
3 shallots, peeled and chopped fine
½ cup lemongrass, chopped fine
6 Kaffir lime leaves, chopped fine
24 green Thai chiles, seeded and chopped
2 tablespoons coriander seeds, toasted and ground
1 teaspoon ground black pepper
½ tablespoon kosher salt
6 tablespoons canola oil
¾ cup cilantro, cut from stem and packed
1 can of coconut milk unsweetened (Taste of Thai brand)

Place all the ingredients except for the cilantro and the coconut milk into the food processor and puree into a paste, then add the cilantro and process until smooth. To create a green curry coconut sauce, whisk the paste with the coconut milk in a small saucepan, bring to a simmer for about 2 minutes, then season to taste with salt. Add more or less curry paste to taste.

Courtesy of Pacifica Seafood Restaurant

Fish

SUGAR-SPICED SALMON

Serves four

Along with the salmon itself, this multistep dish requires preparing a sugar spice rub, a mustard beurre blanc sauce, Chinese long beans, and prepared garlic mashed potatoes.

4 salmon filets, 7 ounces each
½ cup plus 2 tablespoons olive oil
½ cup Sugar Spice Rub, recipe below
¾ cup Mustard Beurre Blanc, recipe below
2 pounds Chinese Long Beans in Black Bean Sauce, recipe follows

Sugar Spice Rub

½ cup sugar
1 teaspoon dry mustard
¼ teaspoon ground cinnamon
¼ tablespoon paprika
2 teaspoons cocoa powder

½ cup chili powder
4 tablespoons ground cumin
1 tablespoon ground black pepper
3 tablespoons kosher salt

Combine all ingredients and mix well.

Mustard Beurre Blanc

1 tablespoon powdered mustard (Colman's brand)
2 tablespoons sugar
2 tablespoons warm water
½ cup beurre blanc

Combine the first 3 ingredients to form a thick paste and mix with the beurre blanc.

Chinese Long Beans in Black Bean Sauce

1 tablespoon sesame oil
1 tablespoon peanut oil
5 tablespoons fresh garlic, minced
Scant ½ cup thinly sliced green onions
1 tablespoon fresh ginger, peeled and minced
¾ cup diced red bell peppers
1½ cups teriyaki sauce
1 cup fermented black beans,
   rinsed well, chopped
3 tablespoons chili garlic paste
2 pounds Chinese long beans

Heat sesame oil and peanut oil and sweat the garlic, green onions, ginger, and peppers. Add the teriyaki sauce, black beans, and chili garlic paste. Simmer for 15 minutes. Heat oil in a wok or sauté pan and gently add the Chinese long beans. Fry for 1-2 minutes until crispy, being careful not to overcook. Toss with black bean sauce to taste.

TO FINISH

Place a large skillet over a medium-high heat and add 3 tablespoons of olive oil. Coat one side of the salmon filet liberally with sugar spice rub, sear for about 2 minutes, then turn over and finish, cooking to desired doneness. To serve, place prepared garlic mashed potatoes in the center of the plate, top with the beans and salmon, and finish by putting the sauce around the edge of the plate.

Courtesy of Pacifica Seafood Restaurant

ROASTED ALASKAN HALIBUT

Serves four

This dish requires preparing the fish as well as a hazelnut froth and artichoke sauté.

4 halibut filets, 7 ounces each
2 teaspoons flour
2 tablespoons canola oil
Hazelnut Froth, recipe below
Artichoke Sauté, recipe follows
Sea salt and white pepper to taste

Season the halibut filets with sea salt and pepper, then dust the flesh side of the halibut with the sifted flour. Heat sauté pan over medium-high heat and add the oil. Place the halibut flour-side down, brown slightly, then place in a preheated 450°F oven for 5-7 minutes. Remove the halibut from the oven and set aside.

• •

Hazelnut Froth

1 Granny Smith apple, peeled, diced   **½ teaspoon coriander seed**
½ onion, small, peeled, diced   **1 cup heavy cream**
2 celery stalks, diced   **Sea salt and white pepper to taste**
½ cup chicken stock   **½ cup hazelnut oil**
1 teaspoon dry mustard
** (Colman's brand)**

Place the apple, onion, and celery in a blender. Add the chicken stock, dry mustard, and coriander, and blend until smooth. Season with sea salt and pepper, then strain through a china cap (a conical strainer used to refine the texture of soups and sauces). Reserve. In small saucepan, reduce the cream by half and set aside. Reserve hazelnut oil to finish the dish.

Chef's Tip

When sautéing fish, use canola oil, as it will not add flavor to the fish. It allows the true flavor of the fish to shine through.

Artichoke Sauté

6 baby artichokes
1 teaspoon canola oil
½ cup alba mushrooms
1 tablespoon butter
1 lemon, zest only
¼ cup hazelnuts, roasted, cut in half
¼ cup parsley, chiffonade
¼ cup baby spinach, chiffonade
Sea salt and freshly ground
** white pepper to taste**

Peel away the outer leaves of the baby artichokes and cut both ends off. Thinly slice the artichokes lengthwise. Add to a heated sauté pan and sauté in canola oil until cooked, then add the mushrooms and continue to sauté. Place in a small saucepan with butter; reserve. Also reserve the remaining ingredients to finish the dish.

To Finish
In a saucepan add the apple puree and reduced cream, and heat, reducing to a sauce consistency. Pour into a large cup and add the hazelnut oil. Blend with a hand blender; season to taste with salt and pepper. Place in a serving dish. In the artichoke saucepan add the lemon zest, hazelnuts, parsley, and spinach; heat and season to taste. To serve, place a small mound of the artichoke mixture in the center of each plate. Place the halibut, flesh side up, on top of the artichoke mixture. Pour the hazelnut froth around the halibut at the table.

Courtesy of Azur, La Quinta Resort & Club

SEARED HAWAIIAN AHI

Serves four

This recipe consists of a mango-papaya relish, avocado puree, and lime beurre blanc sauce.

4 Ahi filets, 7 ounces each
3 teaspoons Togarashi
  (Japanese spice, available at specialty markets)
Mango-Papaya Relish, recipe below
Avocado Puree, recipe follows
Lime Beurre Blanc, recipe follows
Sea salt and white pepper to taste

Mango-Papaya Relish

½ mango, small dice
½ papaya, small dice
1 teaspoon finely diced red pepper
1 teaspoon finely diced yellow pepper
1 tablespoon finely diced Anaheim pepper
½ orange, juice only
½ lime, juice only
1 teaspoon lemon oil
1 teaspoon rice wine vinegar
1 teaspoon honey
Sea salt and white pepper to taste

In a mixing bowl combine the mango, papaya, and peppers. Combine and then add the orange and lime juices. Add the remaining ingredients and mix. Season with salt and pepper; reserve.

Avocado Puree

½ avocado
½ jalapeño, chopped
1 teaspoon cilantro, chopped
1 teaspoon parsley
1 lime, zest only
½ lime, juice only
¼ cup chicken stock

Place everything in a blender and blend until smooth. Push through a fine china cap, season with salt and pepper, and reserve.

Lime Beurre Blanc

1 bottle white wine
1 shallot, minced
1 bay leaf
½ teaspoon whole black pepper
1 tablespoon heavy cream
1 pound butter, cubed, cold
2 lime segments, chopped
Sea salt and white pepper to taste

In a medium saucepan reduce the wine, shallots, bay leaf, and pepper to ¼ cup. Strain the liquid into another saucepan, discarding the shallot mix. Reduce the wine mix by half and add the heavy cream. Over medium heat slowly whip in the cubed butter until fully incorporated, season with salt and pepper, add the lime segments, and keep warm.

TO FINISH

Season the Ahi with salt, pepper, and Togarashi. In hot sauté pan sear the ahi on all sides till rare. With a sharp knife cut the fish into 4-5 even slices. Strain the mango-papaya relish and place a spoonful onto each plate, flatten, and make a rectangle with the relish. With a tablespoon run the avocado puree alongside the relish. Spoon the lime beurre blanc around the relish. Place the seared Ahi on top of the relish.

Courtesy of Azur, La Quinta Resort & Club

LOBSTER TACOS

Serves four (two tacos per person)

4 lobster tails, 6 ounces each
1 tablespoon olive oil
1 head romaine lettuce
16 corn tortillas
2 avocados
½ cup pico de gallo (a chopped relish of tomato, onion, and chiles)
1 lemon
¼ cup Avocado Crema, recipe below
Salt and pepper to taste
8 sprigs cilantro
Mango Pico de Gallo (optional), recipe follows

. . . .

Avocado Crema

1 avocado, pitted, chopped
1 lime, juice only
½ bunch cilantro
1 cup heavy cream
Salt and pepper to taste

In a blender, add avocado, lime juice, and cilantro and blend until smooth. Remove the puree from the blender and place in a mixing bowl; slowly stir heavy cream into avocado mixture. (Do not mix in the blender, or you will "whip" the cream.) Add enough cream to make a dressing-like consistency. Season with salt and pepper. Reserve.

TO FINISH

Remove the lobster tails from the shells and place in mixing bowl. Toss in olive oil, salt, and pepper. Grill lobster until just done and still moist. Heat tortilla stacks (2 per taco). Shred romaine lettuce and place on tortillas. Dress with avocado crema. Cut the lobster tail in chunky pieces, ½ tail per taco. Cut up 2 avocados in a medium dice; add pico de gallo, salt and pepper, and serve on side. Cut lemon into wedges; serve as a garnish with tacos, and top the tacos with cilantro.

Mango Pico de Gallo

1 mango, peeled, pitted, and
  cut into very small dice
½ jalapeño, cut into very small dice
2 tablespoons red onion, minced
  and washed
2 tablespoons red pepper,
  minced and washed
1 lime, juice only
2 tablespoons lemon oil
1 teaspoon honey
2 tablespoons cilantro leaves, minced
Sea salt and white pepper to taste

In a large mixing bowl add the mango,
jalapeño, onion, pepper, lime juice, lemon
oil, honey, and cilantro and mix well.
Season with salt and pepper.

Courtesy of the Viceroy Hotel

Chef's Tip

Lobster, avocado, and mango are excellent together. This recipe for mango pico de gallo can be used in the lobster tacos.

Fish

JOHN DORY WITH BRIOCHE AND TOMATOES

Serves six

6 John Dory filets, 6 ounces each
¼ cup flour
1 tablespoon olive oil
Basil Oil, recipe below
6 Roma tomatoes, roasted, recipe below
Balsamic Dressing, recipe follows
6 slices brioche, lightly toasted
¼ cup balsamic reduction
½ cup rainbow greens for garnish
Salt and white pepper to taste

Basil Oil

½ pound basil leaves
¼ cup extra-virgin olive oil
Salt and white pepper to taste

Blanch the basil leaves and shock in ice, then drain. Process in a food processor; add oil slowly and season with salt and pepper. Reserve.

Roasted Tomatoes

6 Roma tomatoes, sliced ¼ inch thick
2 tablespoons extra-virgin olive oil
Salt and white pepper to taste

Drizzle tomatoes with olive oil. Place the sliced tomatoes on a wire rack, then roast in a preheated 425°F oven for 10 minutes. Sprinkle with salt and pepper. Reserve at room temperature until needed.

Balsamic Dressing

½ cup balsamic vinegar
1 tablespoon garlic, chopped
2 tablespoons basil, julienne
1 cup olive oil
Salt and white pepper to taste

In a blender add vinegar, garlic, and basil and blend for 20 seconds, then slowly add the olive oil. Season with salt and pepper. Reserve.

For balsamic reduction: heat 1 cup balsamic vinegar and simmer gently until reduced to ¼ cup.

TO FINISH
Season the John Dory with salt and pepper and dust with flour. Place a large sauté pan over medium-high heat. Add the olive oil and sauté the fish in the olive oil. Place 4 slices of roasted tomatoes on a metal plate and drizzle with balsamic dressing, then heat in a 425°F oven for 4 minutes. Place one slice of the brioche on the center of the plate and top with the tomatoes, then drizzle the balsamic dressing on the tomatoes, letting it soak through the brioche. Place the fish on top. Drizzle basil oil and balsamic reduction around the fish and top with rainbow mix.

Courtesy of Parker Palm Springs

Fish

DOVER SOLE WITH LEMON SAUCE

Serves four

2 Dover sole filets
1 cup flour
2 lemons, juice only
6 tablespoons butter, unsalted
½ cup white wine
Salt and pepper to taste

Sprinkle the sole with salt and pepper, then roll in the flour; set aside. Place a large skillet over medium-high heat and add 1 tablespoon of the butter. Once the butter is melted, add the sole and quickly sauté on each side, then place in a 450°F oven and bake until done, about 12 minutes. Remove the sole from the oven and de-bone, using tablespoons to lift the meat off of the bone. In a small saucepan, over medium-high heat, cook the remaining butter until brown, then add the white wine and cook for 2 minutes. Add the lemon juice and whisk vigorously until the sauce is thickened; season with salt and pepper. Place the sole filets on dinner plates and spoon the sauce over the top.

Courtesy of Chef Bernard Dervieux, Cuistot Restaurant

Chef's Tip

People often ask if flounder, Pacific sole, sand dabs, or English sole can be substituted for Dover sole. All of these substitute fish are excellent in their own way, but nothing can ever replace the delicate flavor of whole Dover sole.

Fish

CHEF YOSHINORI KOJIMA USED TO BICYCLE TO THE BEACH as a 10-year-old in Japan to make friends with the fishermen and dive for abalone. He was highly motivated: he was hungry. He still has fish flown to him from Tokyo, knowing that the purveyors know him and know that he knows fish. Both of those sets of knowledge are very important.

After starting his career in Hayama, on the coast of Japan, he moved to Los Angeles to work at the Chaya Brasserie there. He has honed his skills and burnished his reputation in several subsequent moves, gaining national attention during a stint in San Francisco where he cooked at the James Beard House as a "rising star of American cuisine." He has settled in the desert at Okura hoping to find the peace to be able to focus on "my cuisine"—more of a philosophical concept than a career ambition.

HAMACHI CARPACCIO WITH SOY-LEMON VINAIGRETTE

Serves four

12 ounces Hamachi, sliced very thin	¼ cup Soy-Lemon Vinaigrette, recipe below
2 tablespoons ginger, minced	Salt and pepper to taste
2 tablespoons chives, minced	
2 tablespoons shallot, minced	

• •

Soy-Lemon Vinaigrette

2 tablespoons lemon juice, fresh squeezed	2 tablespoons extra-virgin olive oil
2 tablespoons soy sauce, low sodium	Salt and pepper to taste

In a mixing bowl combine the soy sauce and lemon juice and then whisk in the olive oil Season with salt and pepper.

Chef's Tip

When eating raw seafood, make sure that the cutting board and all utensils are very clean, and keep the fish refrigerated at all times. Use a chilled plate and be sure to eat the fish immediately after you slice it.

TO FINISH

Place the thinly sliced Hamachi on a chilled plate, covering most of the plate. Sprinkle with the ginger, chive, and shallot, then drizzle the vinaigrette over the fish and season with salt and pepper.

Courtesy of Chef Yoshinori Kojima, Okura Robata Grill & Sushi Bar

DRUNKEN STEAK • FIERY GINGER MARINADE • GARLIC-STUDDED STEAK • COACHELLA STEAK RUB • COCOA-ESPRESSO STEAK RUB • PRIME CERTIFIED ANGUS BEEF PORTERHOUSE • RACK OF LAMB WITH BELUGA LENTIL RAGOUT • BREAST OF DUCK WITH RED WINE RISOTTO AND PARMESAN FROTH • TOOTIE'S SMOKED PORK SPARE RIBS • HOMEMADE SPICE RUB • CREAMED CORN, SAN ANTONIO STYLE • STEAK FRITES • JACK'S BEST EVER SHREDDED PORK OR BEEF SANDWICH • BAJA BUNZ

Meat

High Desert and High Stakes: Meat Dishes

STEAK IS A DEMOCRATIC MEAL; it is prepared at all levels of cooking and sometimes the simplest approach gives the best results. The desert has haute cuisine steak, chain restaurant steak (of assorted grades), and downhome steak, and new steak houses open on a regular basis.

One of the area's most satisfying steak experiences, with its combination of delicious meat and great atmosphere, is at Pappy and Harriet's in Pioneertown, up in the high desert, midway between Palm Springs and Joshua Tree. Pioneertown was originally created in 1946 as a movie set for cowboy movies and television westerns, and Gene Autry and Roy Rogers, as well as many others, worked there. The buildings were made habitable so that the film crews and actors could live there during shooting.

The little town holds a post office (much photographed), a saloon, and a motel. The main street is wide and dusty and could draw you back into childhood fantasies of the West. You could swear you'd seen it before and you probably have, on television.

Even after a recent fire swept the area, Pappy and Harriet's remains an important desert institution. The place draws families, cowboys, bikers and rock musicians. From families to rockers, all devour the steaks, the hamburgers and the chili.

Chris Ward, the chef, swears those steaks are very simple: rubbed with kosher salt, pepper and granulated garlic and thrown on the outdoor grill. "It's the mesquite wood that gives so much flavor," he explains, but it is surely also that sense of being back in an old movie.

77

IF YOU DON'T THINK YOUR OWN OUTDOOR GRILL WILL CONVEY a sense of adventure without extra help, try some of the following rubs and marinades.

DRUNKEN STEAK

2 pounds flank steak
1 cup porter beer, reduced to ½ cup
2 tablespoons Dijon mustard
2 tablespoons honey

3 tablespoons balsamic vinegar
2 cloves garlic, minced
2 tablespoons kosher salt
1 tablespoon cracked black pepper

In a small bowl combine the beer, mustard, honey, balsamic vinegar, and garlic. Place steak in baking pan, pour marinade over it, and toss to coat. Cover with plastic wrap and refrigerate overnight. Remove steak from pan and season with salt and pepper. Grill for 3-5 minutes per side, depending on desired degree of doneness. Slice thinly and serve.

Courtesy of Chef Eric Wadlund, Beefsteak Restaurant

. . . .

FIERY GINGER MARINADE

4 skirt steaks, 6 ounces each
2 tablespoons chili garlic paste
   (Sambal—this is an Indonesian
   condiment made of chili peppers)
3 tablespoons ginger, finely minced
1 tablespoon lemon zest
2 tablespoons garlic, finely minced

2 tablespoons sesame oil
¼ cup canola oil
⅓ cup light brown sugar
½ cup Ponzu (citrus-seasoned
   soy sauce)
2 tablespoons kosher salt
1 tablespoon cracked black pepper

Combine all ingredients for the marinade in a bowl and mix well. Place steaks in marinade for 30–45 minutes. Grill for 3–5 minutes per side, depending on desired degree of doneness.

Courtesy of Chef Eric Wadlund, Beefsteak Restaurant

GARLIC-STUDDED STEAK

4 T-bone steaks, 16 ounces each
6 cloves garlic, peeled and cut into slivers
1 cup extra-virgin olive oil
2 tablespoons chopped fresh rosemary leaves
2 tablespoons kosher salt
1 tablespoon cracked black pepper

With a sharp knife, make several small cuts in the meat, without cutting all the way through. Press a sliver of garlic into each cut. If any garlic is left over, set it aside. In a shallow, nonreactive pan, mix together the olive oil, rosemary, salt, pepper, and any leftover slivers of garlic.

Place steak in the marinade and turn to coat. Let sit at room temperature for ½ hour before grilling. Grill 3–5 minutes per side, depending on desired degree of doneness.

Courtesy of Chef Eric Wadlund, Beefsteak Restaurant

COACHELLA STEAK RUB

¼ cup ancho chili powder
¼ cup Spanish paprika
2 teaspoons chili de arbol powder
2 tablespoons dark brown sugar
1 tablespoon dry mustard
1 tablespoon kosher salt
1 tablespoon ground black pepper
1 tablespoon ground coriander
1 tablespoon dried oregano
1 teaspoon dried cumin

Blend all the ingredients in a mixing bowl. Reserve for use in an airtight container.

Courtesy of Chef Eric Wadlund, Beefsteak Restaurant

Chef's Tip

Make the spice mix and store it in the freezer for freshness.

COCOA-ESPRESSO STEAK RUB

1 tablespoon cocoa powder
1 tablespoon espresso, fine ground, decaf
2 tablespoon finely ground sea salt
1 teaspoon cayenne pepper
½ cup sweet smoked paprika

Blend all the ingredients in a mixing bowl. Reserve for use in an airtight container.

Courtesy of Chef Eric Wadlund, Beefsteak Restaurant

IF YOU WANT HIGH-END, HAUTE CUISINE STEAK—or haute cuisine meat and poultry of any sort—then try your luck at a casino. At Spotlight 29 Casino, to be exact, where there's no luck involved at all in getting a good meal at Rattlesnake. James Beard Award–winning chef Jimmy Schmidt created the menu and keeps an eye on things from his Detroit home base, with occasional visits for special culinary events.

PRIME CERTIFIED ANGUS BEEF PORTERHOUSE

Serves two

2 prime certified Angus porterhouse steaks
2 tablespoons Rattlesnake Steak Seasoning, recipe below
2 dashes olive oil to moisten

2 pinches sea salt
2 sprigs rosemary for garnish
2 servings Rattlesnake 4-sauce selection, recipes follow

Season the steak thoroughly on both sides with Rattlesnake seasoning. Rub the surfaces with olive oil to moisten the spice and affix to the steaks. Cover the steaks with plastic and refrigerate for at least 1 hour. Preheat the grill to high. Remove the steaks from the marinade, draining well. Place the steaks on the grill and sear well for 5 minutes. Turn over to finish cooking to desired temperature, 10–15 minutes, depending on desired degree of doneness. Remove steaks from the grill and allow to rest for a few minutes. Serve on a warm platter garnished with the rosemary and sauces to accompany.

Rattlesnake Steak Seasoning

Makes one cup

¼ cup citrus salt
1 tablespoon garlic salt
¼ cup smoked sea salt
3 tablespoons freshly ground coarse Tellicherry black pepper

3 tablespoons freshly ground coarse Sarawac white pepper
1 teaspoon ground chipotle
1½ teaspoons ground cumin

In a small bowl, combine all the ingredients. Store in an airtight jar for up to one month.

Courtesy of Rattlesnake Restaurant, Spotlight 29 Casino

Chef's Tip

Citrus salt, or sour salt, is used primarily to add tartness to pickling compounds, soups, and sauces. It is produced from the fermentation of crude sugars and lemon or pineapple and is then dehydrated in order to produce water-soluble crystals. It is available in specialty spice stores.

The following four sauces are to be served with the Angus beef porterhouse recipe on the previous page.

* * *

Rattlesnake Mustard Sauce

Makes one cup

1 cup dry white wine
1 cup heavy cream
½ cup whole-grain mustard

1 pinch of sea salt
Dash of Tabasco

In a medium saucepan bring the wine to a boil over high heat; reduce in volume for about 7 minutes. Add the cream, return to a boil, and reduce until thickened to sauce consistency, about 7 minutes. Remove from heat and stir in mustard. Adjust seasoning as necessary with salt and Tabasco, and refrigerate. Warm to serve.

* * *

Rattlesnake Mushroom Ragout

Makes one cup

2 tablespoons olive oil
2 cloves garlic, shaved thin
Red pepper flakes to taste

½ cup field mushrooms, sliced
2 tablespoons Saba wine
Sea salt and black pepper to taste

In a medium nonstick pan, heat the olive oil, garlic, and red pepper flakes over medium heat until tender and translucent, about 8 minutes. Turn the heat to high and add the mushrooms, cooking until seared and all moisture is reduced, about 8 minutes. Remove from heat, season generously with salt and pepper, then stir in the wine and refrigerate. Warm to serve.

Rattlesnake Red Wine Cranberry Sauce

Makes one cup

1 cup fresh cranberries
½ cup light brown sugar
2 cups dry red wine
1 pinch ground allspice
Sea salt and freshly ground
**   black pepper to taste**

In an acid-resistant medium saucepan, combine the cranberries, sugar, and wine and then cook over medium-low heat until the cranberries are softened and translucent, about 15 minutes. Remove from heat. Transfer to a medium sieve and strain to remove the skins and stems. Season with salt, pepper, and ground allspice to taste, and refrigerate. Warm to serve.

Rattlesnake Steak Sauce

Makes one cup

¼ cup Worcestershire sauce
¼ cup A-1 sauce
¼ cup prepared BBQ sauce
1 tablespoon ground preserved ginger
1 tablespoon roasted garlic puree

1 tablespoon aged balsamic vinegar
1 tablespoon low-sodium soy sauce
Dash of chipotle Tabasco to taste
Sea salt to taste

In a small bowl, thoroughly combine all the ingredients, seasoning as necessary with sea salt. Refrigerate. Warm to serve.

Courtesy of Rattlesnake Restaurant, Spotlight 29 Casino

RACK OF LAMB WITH BELUGA LENTIL RAGOUT

Serves four

2 racks of lamb, 8 bones each,
  trimmed and Frenched
2 tablespoons minced garlic
1 teaspoon extra-virgin olive oil
2 cups black beluga lentils
1 cup light vegetable stock
½ cup Picholine or Niçoise olives

1 cup baby artichokes, trimmed
2 red peppers, large, roasted
  and cleaned
4 sage sprigs for garnish
Sea salt and freshly ground black
  pepper to taste

Preheat oven to 400°F. Rub the meat of the lamb with 1 tablespoon of the minced garlic, then season with salt and pepper. Drizzle a couple of drops of olive oil on the meat and rub evenly across the surface to adhere the garlic and spices. Place the roasting pan on a rack in the middle of the oven. Roast the lamb for 10 minutes to sear. Continue cooking at this temperature for rare or medium-rare doneness, or reduce the temperature to 350°F for medium or well-done. Test the roast after 25 minutes with a small instant meat thermometer to determine doneness. Remove meat and allow to rest in a warm spot.

Meanwhile, in a pot of salted boiling water, cook lentils until al dente—tender yet still firm to the bite. Transfer lentils to a colander and drain. In a large nonstick skillet over high heat, add a little olive oil to coat the pan. Add the remaining garlic, cooking until tender and translucent without browning, about 3 minutes. Add the lentils and stock, cooking until the liquids are reduced. Add the artichokes and olives, cooking until warm, then season generously with salt and pepper.

Add the roasted red peppers to a juicer or blender, pureeing until smooth and frothy; season with salt and pepper. Add a little white wine if necessary to adjust the foamy sauce texture.

To Serve
Mound the lentil ragout in the center of warmed bowls. Cut the lamb into double-boned chops. Intertwine the bones of the lamb and position it atop the lentil ragout. Spoon the red pepper foam around the lentil ragout. Garnish with sage and serve.

Courtesy of Rattlesnake Restaurant, Spotlight 29 Casino

Chef's Tip

Black beluga lentils glisten when they're cooked, which makes them look like beluga caviar. They are also great in soups or salads or served with fish. French green lentils could also be used as a substitute.

BREAST OF DUCK WITH RED WINE RISOTTO AND PARMESAN FROTH

Serves four

4 duck breasts, 8 ounces each, trimmed of excess fat
4 slices duck foie gras
1 bottle dry red wine, preferably Syrah or Merlot
¼ cup honey
1 tablespoon olive oil
4 shallots, large, peeled and diced fine
1½ cups Violone Nano or Arborio rice
3½ cups vegetable stock or light poultry stock, hot
¼ cup parmesan cheese, finely grated
4 tablespoons butter, unsalted
½ cup micro greens or herbs for garnish
2 tablespoons chive oil for garnish
Sea salt and freshly ground black pepper to taste

Parmesan Froth

½ cup skim milk, steamed and frothy
¼ cup Parmigiano-Reggiano cheese, finely grated

In a large acid-resistant saucepan combine the red wine (reserving ½ cup for the risotto) and the honey. Bring to a simmer over high heat, cooking until reduced to ½ cup volume. Remove from the heat and reserve. In a nonstick skillet over low heat cook the seasoned duck breasts, skinside down, until browned and fat rendered, about 15 minutes. Remove from heat and reserve.

To make the risotto: In a large saucepan, over medium-high heat the olive oil. Add the shallots and cook for 4 minutes. Add the rice and cook until warm to the back of the hand, about 3 minutes. Add the reserved ½ cup red wine to the rice and allow the wine to evaporate. Add 2 cups of the hot stock and bring to a simmer, stirring frequently. Add salt to taste. Cook the rice until the liquid has reduced to coat the rice, about 6 minutes. Add about ¾ cup of the stock and allow it to reduce to coat the rice, 3–4 minutes. Repeat,

Chef's Tip

To give this recipe a truly California feel use Sonoma foie gras. Moulard duck breasts (magrets) are more flavorful and larger than regular duck breasts since they come from a duck that has produced foie gras.

adding small amounts of the hot stock until the rice becomes quite creamy yet still al dente (firm to the bite) and nearly all the liquid is used. Add the last of the stock and the reduced red wine, cooking until creamy and thickened. Adjust the seasoning with salt and pepper to taste. Remove from heat. Add ¼ cup parmesan cheese and the butter, stirring to combine. Spoon immediately into warm, rimmed soup bowls.

Once the risotto is started, return the skillet to the burner over high heat. Add the duck and transfer to the lower rack of a 400°F oven to finish cooking, 5–8 minutes, depending on size. Remove from the oven and transfer the duck to a plate, allowing it to rest 3 minutes before slicing.

Return the pan to high heat—remember the handle may still be hot from the oven. Add the foie gras, cooking until well seared, about 1 minute. Turn over and finish cooking for another minute, depending on the thickness of the foie gras. Transfer to the duck holding plate. With a very sharp, thin knife cut the duck into thin slices width-wise, or against the grain. Stack the sliced duck artistically in the center of the risotto, then position the foie gras atop the duck. Mound the micro herbs atop the foie gras. Combine the steamed milk and ¼ cup of Parmigiano-Reggiano cheese, frothing with a hand blender. Spoon the froth around the edges of the risotto, then drizzle the chive oil over the foam. Serve immediately.

Courtesy of Rattlesnake Restaurant,
Spotlight 29 Casino

Meat

IN 2003 *SUNSET* MAGAZINE SET OUT TO FIND THE BEST BARBECUE in the West. To the delight of all desert barbecue lovers, but not to their surprise, one of the ten best in the state of California turned out to be Willard Sterling and Steven Vinson's East Texas barbecue at Tootie's, a small, unpretentious, but flavor-packed restaurant in Cathedral City. Tootie's is now in *Sunset's* "Barbecue Hall of Fame."

TOOTIE'S SMOKED PORK SPARE RIBS

Serves four

2 sides pork spare ribs
½ cup Homemade Spice Rub, recipe follows
½ cup barbecue sauce

Ask your butcher for 2 "down" pork spare ribs. These are cut 2 down off the brisket, which yields smaller and meatier ribs. Trim excess fat off both sides. Also trim excess end meat (without bone) to prevent burning. (Some believe the thin membrane on the backside of the ribs needs to be removed for a more tender rib. However, the indirect "low and slow" cooking method makes this extra step unnecessary.)

The night before, season both sides of the ribs with your favorite dry rub—we use a rub that is made for Tootie's Texas barbecue by Texas Coffee Company in Beaumont, Texas (800-259-3400 or www.texiov.com). Lightly sprinkle a medium chili powder on the top (meat side) of the rack. This gives it a nice mahogany appearance, as well as a little snap to the flavor. Wrap and refrigerate.

The smoker used at the restaurant consists of an eight-rack rotisserie with a convection fan and a firebox on the side. This method bathes the meat evenly in smoke (we use green oak) while cooking the meat at a low temperature over a long period of time.

With your home smoker, maintain a chamber temperature between 225° and 250°F. Achieve this by adjusting vents or by adding more wood. Place the ribs on the rack(s) meat-side up. If you do not have a firebox, place the ribs away from any direct heat. Cook for about 3 hours, then flip over to bone side up for 30-60 minutes. Then flip to meat-side up and cook for another 1–1½ hours.

Check for doneness by lifting the ribs from the center. The ribs should bow and the meat should start to crack on the top surface. You should also see the rib bones exposed on the end. East Texas–style barbecue never sauces the meat while it is cooking. The sauce is treated like a gravy and used as a complement to the finely smoked meat as it is served.

Courtesy of Chef Willard Sterling,
Tootie's Texas Barbecue

Chef's Tip

If you want to make your own dry rub, here is a quick recipe:

HOMEMADE SPICE RUB

2 tablespoons light brown sugar
2 tablespoons smoked paprika
2 tablespoons spicy chili powder

1 teaspoon mustard powder
1 teaspoon ground mace
Salt and black pepper to taste

Blend all ingredients in a mixing bowl. Store in an airtight container.

Meat

ONE OF TOOTIE'S MOST POPULAR SIDE ORDERS is their San Antonio–style creamed corn. Okay, it's not a meat recipe, but we didn't think it should be separated too far from Tootie's ribs. A good match should not be split up.

CREAMED CORN, SAN ANTONIO STYLE

Serves six

1½ cups creamed corn
1½ cups whole corn, frozen
2 tablespoons butter, unsalted
1 tablespoon flour
½ cup minced onion

1 cup whole milk, scalded
1 tablespoon jalapeño, diced, canned
1 teaspoon jalapeño juice
Salt to taste

To begin, make a béchamel sauce by placing a saucepan over medium heat and adding 1½ tablespoons of butter. Once the butter is melted, whip in the flour and continue to cook for about 2 minutes. Add the scalded milk and continue whipping for 3–5 minutes, until the mixture is smooth and thickened. Set aside but keep warm. Then place a sauté pan over medium heat and add remaining butter and onions and sauté until soft, but do not brown. Add the sautéed onions, creamed corn, whole corn, diced jalapeños, and jalapeño juice to the béchamel sauce. Season the creamed corn with salt and cook over medium-high heat for 5 minutes, stirring frequently.

Courtesy of Chef Willard Sterling,
Tootie's Texas Barbecue

Chef's Tip

Sauce béchamel is a sauce named after Louis de Béchamel, a seventeenth-century French financier. It is one of the five mother sauces. The use of scalded milk will help to prevent lumping.

However adventurous a restaurant may be, the odds are that steak will be the most popular thing on the menu. Citron has always prided itself on the global scope and cosmopolitanism of its dishes, but steak frites remains its most ordered item. The truffle vinaigrette gives an extra spin to a classic.

Steak Frites

Serves four

4 New York strip steaks, 10 ounces each
4 russet potatoes
1 pound baby spinach
½ cup cherry tomatoes, cut in half

¼ cup crumbled Herb blue cheese
¼ cup Lemon Vinaigrette (see page 27)
¼ cup Truffle Vinaigrette, recipe below
Salt and pepper to taste

• •

Truffle Vinaigrette

Scant ½ cup black truffle shavings
½ cup truffle oil
¼ cup plus 1 tablespoon white
  wine vinegar

Salt and pepper to taste
¼ cup plus 1 tablespoon olive oil

In a blender, add black truffles, truffle oil, vinegar, salt, and pepper. Blend until smooth. Add olive oil to create an emulsion.

To Finish
Season steaks with salt and pepper and set aside. Cut the ends off the potatoes, cut them in half, then in half again (until you have 4 rectangular "sticks" per potato). Fry in a 350°F fryer until golden brown. Remove the frites from the fryer and place them in a bowl; season with salt and pepper. While the frites are cooking, place the steak on a very hot grill and grill to the desired temperature. Toss the frites with truffle vinaigrette and stack criss-cross on the serving plate.

Place the steak on the plate. In a large mixing bowl toss the spinach, blue cheese, and cherry tomatoes with just enough lemon vinaigrette to dress the salad, then place on the plate.

Courtesy of Citron Restaurant, Viceroy Hotel

Chef's Tip

A great blue cheese to use for this is the Maytag Blue made in Iowa. The cheese was created at Maytag Dairy Farms by Fred Maytag II, the son of the Maytag washer company founder E. H. Maytag.

91

JACK LAROCH STARTED HIS WORKING LIFE AS A CHEF, but the hours didn't fit in with his idea of family life. He wished to spend more time with his baby daughter and he wanted to be home at night and on weekends. So he took a 9–5 job and cooked in his spare time. His cooking actually became part of an extended family life. Jack cooked barbecue for his daughter's birthday parties, which became a family tradition. Friends and relatives told him that he should bottle his barbecue sauce commercially, and by the time he had reached her 18th birthday party, he started thinking about it seriously. Now Jack's BBQ Sauce is known far wider than Indio, where he lives, and far beyond the Coachella Valley.

LaRoch sent samples to TV weatherman Al Roker when he saw Roker tasting barbecue on television. "That guy understands barbecue," LaRoch decided. Al Roker certainly understood Jack's sauce. He featured it in *Al Roker's Big Bad Book of Barbecue*, and asked LaRoch to send 200 bottles of his Cowboy Ketchup to give away at his book party. (The barbecue sauce comes in three levels of heat: the Original, Cowboy Ketchup, and Smok'n Hot.) LaRoch and his family were invited to attend the party, a star-studded Manhattan event. LaRoch has been asked to expand, but he's not quite ready for that. That might *really* take too much time away from his family.

JACK'S BEST EVER SHREDDED PORK OR BEEF SANDWICH

1 pound beef chuck or pork butt, cut in 2-inch pieces
16-ounce can chicken or beef stock
Jack's Original, Cowboy Ketchup, or Smok'n Hot Sauce

Place meat and broth in a lightly greased baking dish that can be sealed well with foil. Cover with foil and bake at 400°F for 15 minutes. Reduce heat to 325°F. Bake for 2 hours. Remove the pan from the oven; open carefully—it will be hot. The meat should be falling apart; if not, reseal and cook a little longer. When it is cooked, drain the liquid from the pan and then shred the meat with two forks. Coat the meat with Jack's Original, Cowboy Ketchup, or Smok'n Hot Sauce while it is still hot. You can make sandwiches immediately or cool to room temperature. After cooling, the meat can be refrigerated for 1–2 days or frozen for future use; it actually tastes better after marinating. Serve on heated buns.

Courtesy of Jack LaRoch

HAMBURGERS MUST BE THE MOST BASIC sort of meat dish to serve, but at Bunz the young owner tries to create some surprises as well as delivering the tried and true. The daughter of a prominent local caterer, she knows enough not to play things too safe.

BAJA BUNZ

Serves four

4 certified Angus beef patties, 8 ounces each
¼ cup chopped cilantro
1 bunch green onion
½ cup Ortega chiles, diced
4 tablespoons mayonnaise
4 tablespoons ketchup
1 tablespoon mustard
8 leaves lettuce
8 slices tomato
1 dill pickle, quartered
8 slices onion, thinly sliced
8 slices pepperjack cheese
8 jalapeño cheese kaiser buns

Cook the meat on a charcoal grill with a dash of salt and pepper. Sauté the cilantro, green onion, and Ortega chiles and place on top of the meat, between two pieces of cheese. Steam or grill the bun to your perfection. Spread mayo on both top and bottom of bun, then a ring of ketchup on the top bun and a ring of mustard on the bottom bun. Place cooked meat on top of bottom bun. Next add the cheese, leaf of lettuce, a fresh slice of tomato, onions, pickle and the top bun.

Courtesy of Jaclyn Peña

Meat

93

PIMM'S ROYALE • APPLE STRUDEL • RASPBERRY LEMON-LIME DROP MARTINI • MELVYN'S COFFEE • SAKE TO ME • LEMONCELLO MARTINI • VICEROY POPSICLE TINI • SUNSET MARTINI • WELCOME DRINK • ORANGE BLOSSOM MARGARITA

Drinks

Drinks in the Desert

PALM SPRINGS FIRST BECAME KNOWN as a healthy place to bring well-to-do invalids; the air was good for their chests and the hot springs were good for their aches and pains.

But the future for hoteliers clearly lay in a more general appeal and by 1915 the hospitality business flourished, greatly helped by the movie industry. The desert was also an ideal place for filmmakers to come when they needed locations for stories set in Arabia, or Mexico, or the Wild West. In the early 1920s many silent movies were shot here; William Powell, the urbane star of the *Thin Man* movies, first came to the desert playing cowboy villains in silent westerns.

It was the Racquet Club, a tennis and social club founded by actor Ralph Bellamy and silent movie star Charles Farrell, that brought national attention. It opened in December 1934 with four tennis courts, a swimming pool, and – even more importantly – the Bamboo bar, where many Hollywood stories began. There were no accommodations – bungalows were added later due to popular movie star demand.

Farrell, an enthusiastic tennis player, also liked to drink, as did most of the Racquet Club members. Bing Crosby, a club habitué, would happily sing for the crowd when asked, and used to add to his act by wandering through the audience with a bottle of Glenlivet in his hand, generously pouring the single malt into the glasses of the guests – no matter what they happened to be drinking. One local legend states that the Bloody Mary was created here, as a much needed hangover cure. Farrell is also reputed to have introduced Pimm's Cup to America after discovering the drink when filming in England in 1937. The club held an annual Pimm's Cup tennis tournament: Ginger Rogers and her partner won the first mixed doubles, defeating Gorgeous Gussie Moran and her partner.

95

PIMM'S ROYALE

Pimm's is generally served with sparkling lemonade or with ginger ale, one part Pimm's to three parts lemonade or ginger ale. But in the Racquet Club tradition of high living and high alcohol consumption, try it with champagne.

Pimm's No. 1
Champagne
Strawberries

Pour Pimm's No. 1 into a champagne flute and top with chilled champagne. Garnish with slices of strawberry to enhance the fruit flavor and add to the festivity.

. . . .

APPLE STRUDEL

⅛ cup apple schnapps	
1 teaspoon cinnamon schnapps	1 splash apple juice
1 teaspoon white Crème de Cacao	⅛ cup whipped heavy cream
1 teaspoon dark Crème de Cacao	1 pinch cinnamon

Mix schnapps, Crème de Cacao, and apple juice in a shaker. Pour into a martini glass, top with whipped heavy cream, and sprinkle cinnamon on top.

Courtesy of Chef Johannes Bacher, Johannes' Restaurant

RASPBERRY LEMON-LIME DROP MARTINI

2 tablespoons raspberry vodka
2 tablespoons Citron vodka
1 tablespoon Triple Sec
1 tablespoon Chambord

¼ fresh squeezed lemon
¼ fresh squeezed lime
1 sugar packet for garnish

Sugarcoat the rim of a chilled martini glass. Add the ingredients into a shaker with ice and shake. Strain into martini glass.

Courtesy of Twenty 6, La Quinta Resort & Club

THE DESERT INN HAS BEEN TORN DOWN; and the El Mirador, a local landmark, has become a hospital; and the Racquet Club is closed, perhaps to be reopened after extensive development and restoration of the property. But farther east one of the oldest desert resorts still thrives. The La Quinta Resort opened in 1926 and it became a favorite sanctuary for such peace-loving pioneer movie directors as Frank Capra and Dorothy Arzner, who kept bungalows on the grounds. It was known for its discretion and quickly became a hideaway for those who needed to keep their romances out of the public eye.

"If someone was having a blazing affair that was either illegal, scandalous, bad box office, or against their Studio's orders, off they flitted to the desert and 'hidden' La Quinta," recalled Maria Riva, Marlene Dietrich's daughter, looking back to her mother's own trips there.

Today the resort regularly entertains golf and tennis stars as well as Hollywood names. The place is still discreet, and those who don't want to be seen can stay by their private pools behind high walls or perhaps snatch a semipublic moment in the dark banquettes at the back of the resort's bar-restaurant. Named "Twenty 6" in honor of the resort's birth date, it is an ideal spot to have drinks on the patio, by the waterfall. It's a good way to start or end an evening—if you're not trying to avoid public scrutiny.

Drinks MELVYN'S COFFEE

2 tablespoons Frangelico	¾ cup coffee
2 tablespoons Bailey's Irish Cream	¼ cup whipped cream

In a 7-ounce continental coffee glass pour the Frangelico and the Bailey's, then fill the glass with coffee. Top with whipped cream.

Courtesy of Melvyn's Restaurant, Ingleside Inn

THE INGLESIDE INN WAS FIRST TRANSFORMED into a small, exclusive hotel in the mid-thirties. Ava Gardner dined and drank here, and Howard Hughes, and a host of stars and movie industry people before and after them. The owner, Ruth Hardy, made disapproving notes about many of her clientele in her private index. Some were morally lower than a good hotelkeeper would wish, some (the Goldwyns, for example) were of the wrong ethnic origin, but making the notes must have assuaged her feelings: they don't seem to have been turned away.

After Ruth Hardy's death in 1965, the place languished for a while, but when Mel Haber bought it in 1975 he brought an enthusiasm that revived its fortunes. Romance was often in the air and marriage sometimes came along too. June Allyson highly recommended getting married at the Inn at least once in a lifetime. Frank Sinatra and the Rat Pack hung out at the Ingleside Inn; Sinatra held his 1976 prewedding supper at Melvyn's.

Diners still propose here so often that staff don't even turn a hair when an ardent swain drops to his knees in the middle of the dining room. The bar is lined with several photographs of the great, the famous, and the momentarily celebrated who relaxed here. If any place still holds an aura of old-time glamour, it's Melvyn's and the Ingleside Inn.

SAKE TO ME

3 tablespoons cucumber vodka
2 tablespoons sake
1 tablespoon lemon–lime mix
1 splash ginger syrup
2 pieces pickled ginger

In a martini shaker mix vodka, sake, and lemon-lime mix. Coat a martini glass rim twice around with the ginger syrup. Place pickled ginger in the glass. Pour the martini over it.

*Courtesy of Chef Johannes Bacher,
Johannes Restaurant*

Chef's Tip

To infuse the vodka with cucumber flavor, peel two cucumbers and cut into spears. Place the spears in an empty liter bottle, then fill the bottle with the vodka of your choice. This should take about ½ liter of vodka. Leave for 24 hours, then taste.

You can prepare vodkas in this way with any flavor you like: try jalapeño peppers (only place a few in the bottom of the bottle until you have determined the degree of heat you prefer) or herbs. Johannes makes coffee vodka in this way by putting a layer of coffee beans in the bottom of the bottle and adding the vodka.

LEMONCELLO MARTINI

¼ cup Lemoncello
⅛ cup vodka

In a martini shaker, shake Lemoncello and vodka. Pour into a martini glass, and serve with lemon twist.

Courtesy of Chef Johannes Bacher,
Johannes Restaurant

THE MARTINI, H. L. Mencken once declared, is the only American invention as perfect as the sonnet. Where, how, and by whom it was invented are all matters of debate. But by some cosmic coincidence martinis have been at their peak of popularity exactly at the times when the desert was also fashionable—in the 1930s (an ironic result of Prohibition and the rise of bathtub gin); the 1950s, when martinis ruled as king of the cocktail parties; and today, when the chic have rediscovered the charms of mid-century style. The most cutting-edge cocktails are to be found at Citron, the bar and restaurant at the Viceroy Hotel in Palm Springs, or at Johannes Restaurant, where some of the best food in the valley is also served.

VICEROY POPSICLE TINI

2 tablespoons fresh watermelon purée
1 tablespoon Grey Goose vodka
Popsicle, recipe below

Combine ingredients in a shaker with ice. Shake, strain into a martini glass, and finish with a popsicle.

Popsicle

Fresh grapefruit juice
Fresh lime juice
Fresh mint

Mix ingredients in a blender. Freeze in a popsicle maker.

Courtesy of Citron Restaurant, the Viceroy Hotel

WATCHING THE SUN GO DOWN, SIPPING A COCKTAIL, is a favorite desert pastime. The Cliffhouse Restaurant, with views facing west across the whole valley, has been a favorite location for sunset watching for the last decade.

SUNSET MARTINI

3 Ketel One vodka
1 tablespoon peach schnapps

1 splash cranberry juice
1 splash orange juice

Combine vodka, schnapps, and cranberry juice in a shaker with ice. Shake, strain into a martini glass, and finish with a splash of orange juice.

Courtesy of the Cliffhouse Restaurant

WELCOME DRINK

6–7 mint leaves, muddled
2 tablespoons Pomegranate Syrup, recipe below
3 tablespoons Hangar One vodka
¼ cup tonic
¼ cup soda water
garnish with lime

Begin with muddled (crushed) mint leaves in the bottom of the glass. The crushing releases mint oil into the mixture. Pour pomegranate syrup into the glass, add vodka, fill with tonic and soda, stir, and garnish.

Pomegranate Syrup

3 bottles pomegranate juice, 16 ounces each
1 orange
2 limes
1 lemon
4 star anise
1 teaspoon black peppercorns
1 piece of fresh ginger, 1–1½ inches
1 cup sugar
1 cup orange juice

Pour pomegranate juice into a stockpot. Cut fruit in halves and add to pot. Add spices, sugar, juice, and cut up the ginger (no need to peel it). Bring to a boil and reduce by half. Strain and refrigerate.

Courtesy of the Viceroy Hotel

Chef's Tip

This may seem like a lot of pomegranate syrup, but you can store it indefinitely, thanks to the acid of the citrus. It can also be mixed with vodka or champagne.

102

ORANGE BLOSSOM MARGARITA

3 tablespoons José Cuervo 1800 tequila
1 tablespoon Cointreau
1 splash sweet-and-sour mix
1 splash orange juice

Combine ingredients in blender, blend,
and pour into a margarita glass. Garnish
with an orange slice.

Courtesy of the Cliffhouse Restaurant

THE GRAZING PLATE • QUAIL STUFFED WITH PANCETTA AND SWEETBREADS • CHICKEN "MQUALLI" WITH PRESERVED LEMON • BROILED HALIBUT ON PINEAPPLE SAUERKRAUT • VEAL CHOP GRAND MÈRE (GRANDMOTHER STYLE) • CARBONNADES FLAMANDES (BELGIAN BEEF STEW) • BRAISED FREE-RANGE RABBIT WITH SPANISH ONIONS AND PEPPERS • VEAL SCALOPPINI WITH MUSHROOMS AND DRY WHITE VERMOUTH • CHICKEN TANDOORI WITH SHRIMP AND MANGO • BIG-EYE TUNA TARTAR • CRISPY FRIED SOFT-SHELL CRAB WITH SPICY SESAME MISO

International Cuisine

Coming to the Desert: International Cuisine

WHEN THE *DESERT SUN'S* MONTHLY MAGAZINE, *DESERT MAGAZINE*, published its first special food issue half a decade ago, I was the editor. I got a semicomplimentary, semicritical phone call from a part-time resident who lived the rest of the time in San Francisco. She was troubled because she'd enjoyed reading the issue but believed it raised false hopes. The desert, she felt, was doomed to disappoint her and foodies like her; apart from one or two star chefs who artificially raised the standard, food in the Coachella Valley, she said, was not what she had learned to expect in San Francisco.

San Francisco holds the rest of America to a very high standard, so I could understand her concern. At the same time I thought she was blind to the extraordinary advances that were being made in the valley. Food, I've always believed, is like theatre; it requires an educated audience to appreciate the work or the work can't thrive. Over the last five years that audience has been arriving (a large proportion of it made up of San Franciscans looking for cheaper real estate and better weather).

It began with the boutique hotels, catering to an international clientele. A chef at Citron, the restaurant in the Viceroy Hotel in Palm Springs, once told me that a major appeal of working there was that many of the hotel guests formed just such an educated audience. Their standards had been set eating in San Francisco, New York, Paris, Barcelona, or London, and they weren't going to lower those standards when they were in the desert. Citron keeps its menu fairly simple, but it's a sophisticated simplicity.

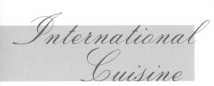

THE GRAZING PLATE

Serves four

3 cups Hummus, recipe below
2 cups olives, mixed blend
¼ pound prosciutto, sliced very thin
8 pieces grilled bread,
   cut into long pieces

8 slices tomato
¼ cup balsamic vinegar
¼ cup olive oil
⅛ cup paprika oil

Arrange the hummus, olives, prosciutto, tomatoes, and bread artfully on plates. Serve the oils and balsamic vinegar in ramekins on the side for dipping.

• •

Hummus

2 pounds chickpeas (garbanzo beans)
2 cloves garlic, roasted
⅓ cup tahini

3 tablespoons lemon juice
¼ cup olive oil
Salt and pepper to taste

Place all of the ingredients in a food processor and puree until smooth; season with salt and pepper.

Courtesy of Citron Restaurant, Viceroy Hotel

Chef's Tip

You can spice up regular olives with chili flakes, lemon zest, bay leaf, and rosemary.

THE CHEFS AND RESTAURANT OWNERS ARRIVED IN THE VALLEY, too. Le Vallauris in Palm Springs and its sibling restaurant, Le St. Germain in Indian Wells, planted the French flag in the area. Cuistot Restaurant in Palm Desert, created by Chef Bernard Dervieux, has links to the greatest French tradition; Dervieux apprenticed with the legendary Paul Bocuse in Lyon and later worked with the almost equally acclaimed Roger Vergé in the south of France. Dervieux designed his landmark building to pay homage to the French farmhouse he himself grew up in; the place is a culinary landmark as well as a geographical one. Chef Dervieux has long been regarded as a leading contender for the reputation of finest chef in the desert.

QUAIL STUFFED WITH PANCETTA AND SWEETBREADS

Serves four

8 quail
½ cup Pancetta Sweetbread Stuffing, recipe below
¼ cup plus 2 tablespoons butter, unsalted

1 cup chicken stock
¼ cup white wine
1 bay leaf
2 cups brown rice, cooked, warm
Salt and pepper to taste

Pancetta Sweetbread Stuffing

1 tablespoon butter, unsalted
½ cup pancetta, diced small and cooked

½ cup sweetbreads, diced small
2 tablespoons shallots, minced
Salt and pepper to taste

Place a large skillet over medium-high heat, then add the butter, pancetta, sweetbreads, and shallots. Sauté; season with salt and pepper. Remove from the heat and cool.

Continued on next page

To Finish

Stuff the quail with pancetta stuffing and season with salt and pepper. Place a large skillet over medium-high heat and add 2 tablespoons of butter. Place the quail skin side down and sauté until browned on both sides. Reduce the heat to low and cover; continue cooking until cooked through. Remove the quail and set aside, keeping warm. In the skillet add the stock, wine, and bay leaf. Return to medium-high heat and reduce by two-thirds, then whip in the remaining butter to make the sauce. Turn off the heat. Place the rice in the middle of the plate and then slice the quail into 3 pieces each; place 2 quail on the rice, spoon the sauce over the quail, and serve immediately.

Courtesy of Chef Bernard Dervieux, Cuistot Restaurant

Chef's Tip

Pancetta, or Italian bacon, is cured with salt and spices but not smoked. Flavorful and slightly salty, pancetta comes in a sausage-like roll. The best way to cook it is to slice the pancetta very thin and lay it out on a jellyroll pan, then at 350°F until crisp. Remove from the oven and place the cooked pancetta on paper towels. Once it is cool, chop the pancetta.

CHICKEN "MQUALLI" WITH PRESERVED LEMON

2 chickens, about 3 pounds each, cut into pieces
1 teaspoon fresh ginger, grated
1 teaspoon olive oil
1 pinch of saffron
2 teaspoons peanut oil
1 tablespoon butter
2 onions, thinly sliced
1 clove of garlic, crushed
One peel of a preserved lemon, cut into quarters

Place the chicken pieces in a saucepan, and add oils, butter, ginger, onion, garlic, saffron, and 2 cups of water. Cover and bring to a boil, then turn the chicken, stir to mix the spices, and leave to cook over moderate heat. Keep an eye on the sauce as it reduces, adding a little water if necessary. Turn the chicken over from time to time until it is well covered with sauce. When the chicken is ready (the meat will easily be detached), add the preserved lemon peel. Leave to simmer for a few minutes, taste, and serve.

Courtesy of Hedi Hamrouni, Hedi's Cafe Paris

JOHANNES BACHER WAS BORN AND GREW UP IN AUSTRIA but his cooking career has taken him all over the world. When he first came to the desert, he brought with him a cosmopolitan flair that made him an immediate sensation. At that time fusion cooking was a new trend and Bacher was its pioneer in the Coachella Valley. His cosmopolitanism is an essential part of his approach to food, but now he has also gone back to his roots, presenting Austrian cooking in a contemporary way—lighter but still rich in flavors. His reputation in the Valley rivals Dervieux's and his menu is always an adventure.

BROILED HALIBUT ON PINEAPPLE SAUERKRAUT

Serves four

This recipe requires preparing roasted potatoes, sausage, pineapple sauerkraut, and a passion fruit and mango mustard sauce.

4 Alaskan halibut fillets, 7 ounces each
2 tablespoons grapeseed oil
4 habanero chicken sausages
8 Roasted Potatoes,
   recipe below

¾ cup Pineapple Sauerkraut,
   recipe follows
¾ cup Passion Fruit and Mango
   Mustard Sauce, recipe follows
Salt and pepper to taste

Place a large sauté pan over medium-high heat and add the grapeseed oil. Sear the halibut, then move the pan to a 425°F oven. Cook for 6 minutes or until medium done. In a skillet over medium heat, cook the sausage until evenly brown. Cool and slice.

Roasted Potatoes

8 fingerling potatoes
Olive oil

Salt to taste

Preheat the oven to 425°F. Peel potatoes and place them in a saucepan of water. Bring to a boil and simmer for 10 minutes. Drain. Coat bottom of a shallow pan with olive oil. Place cooked potatoes in the pan, sprinkle with salt to taste, and roast for 20 minutes. Serve warm.

Pineapple Sauerkraut

2 cups sauerkraut, Claussen brand,
    drained and rinsed
1 onion, small dice
2 tablespoons butter
1 bay leaf
1 potato, small, grated
¾ cup pineapple, small dice
1 teaspoon sugar or honey
1 tablespoon heavy cream
1 tablespoon crème fraîche
1 tablespoon caraway seed
1 cup sparkling wine
Salt and pepper to taste

Place a saucepot over medium heat; then add the butter and sauté the onion until golden, then add the sauerkraut and sauté for 2 minutes, stirring constantly. Add the remaining ingredients and braise until tender; season with salt and pepper.

Passion Fruit and Mango Mustard Sauce

½ pound mango puree
½ pound passion fruit puree
1½ cups heavy cream

1 tablespoon crème fraîche
½ cups mirin (a sweet rice wine)

1 tablespoon mustard, whole-grain
Salt and pepper to taste

In a large saucepan add all ingredients and reduce until it reaches a sauce consistency. Season with salt and pepper.

TO SERVE

Place a 4-inch ring mold in the middle of a dinner plate; put the sauerkraut in the mold, pat down, and then remove the mold. Spoon the sauce around the plate. Cut the potatoes into 3 pieces and arrange around the plate. Finish by placing the halibut on top of the sauerkraut, with the sliced sausage on the right.

Courtesy of Chef Johannes Bacher, Johannes Restaurant

WE'RE LUCKY IN THE DESERT because we not only have French food at the haute cuisine level, we also have some of the best French bistro food anywhere. Chef Pierre Pelech was born in the south of France, in Pau. He learned his craft in the south of France and on the Riviera. His flavors are still influenced by that background, though he has also worked in the Caribbean, in Polynesia, and for 20 years owned a restaurant, the Los Feliz Inn, in Los Angeles. He uses his "Specials" board like the most creative of teachers, inspiring his customers to try dishes that, without his seductive influence, they might otherwise shy away from. It's like eating at one of the best bistros in France, but without any tourist's angst.

Five years ago no one could have confidently foretold how many ambitious new restaurants would open in the valley, or just how diverse they would be. At Zin American Bistro, Belgian-born chef Nicholas Klontz rings the changes on his bistro theme by highlighting a different cuisine from month to month—the basic menu remains, but with his specials he visits a new shore of the Mediterranean as his fancy takes him. His fancy is based on rich experience; like Bernard Dervieux, he has worked with Roger Vergé in the south of France, and in Spain he cooked in the kitchen of Restaurante Arzak, where Juan Mari Arzak and his daughter Elena have won acclaim as leaders of the new Spanish cuisine. In Palm Desert at La Spiga, Vince Cultraro serves classic Italian at its best, while close by Hedi Hamrouni draws on his Tunisian roots with a French/Moroccan/Tunisian menu. At Copley's on Palm Canyon, British chef Andrew Copley brings an eclectic touch that frequently echoes his experiences cities like London, Australia, San Francisco, and Hawaii. In La Quinta, at Okura, Japanese cuisine is treated with the elegance it deserves.

VEAL CHOP GRAND MÈRE (GRANDMOTHER STYLE)

Serves four

24 button mushrooms	4 veal chops, 12 ounces each
½ cup white wine	2 cups veal stock
24 pearl onions	24 pieces bacon, diced, cooked
2 tablespoons olive oil	2 tablespoons shallots, minced

In a large sauté pan cook the mushrooms in the white wine. Remove mushrooms from the pan, keep warm, and reserve wine. In another large sauté pan add half of the olive oil and sauté the pearl onions over medium heat until golden brown. Remove the onions from the pan and keep warm.

Place a large sauté pan over medium-high heat; add the veal chops and brown on both sides to a deep golden brown. Add the shallots and deglaze with the mushroom-flavored white wine. Add the veal stock and bring to a boil. Bake at 375°F for 10–15 minutes or until medium done. Remove from the oven and remove the veal from the pan. Add the bacon, mushrooms, and onions to the veal stock; place over medium-high heat and reduce to sauce consistency. Serve with roasted or mashed potatoes.

Courtesy Chef Pierre Pelech, Chez Pierre Bistro

Chef's Tip

Place any leftover veal stock in ice cube trays and keep in a freezer. Pull out a couple of veal cubes as needed. This technique also works very well with extra tomato paste.

CARBONNADES FLAMANDES (BELGIAN BEEF STEW)

Serves six

3¾ pounds beef, suitable for braising (round or chuck steak)
1 slice whole-grain country-style bread
2 tablespoons Dijon mustard
1 tablespoon vegetable oil
2 tablespoons butter, unsalted
1½ pounds Spanish onions, sliced thin
1 pound carrots, sliced
3 tablespoons raspberry preserves
2 tablespoons red wine vinegar
2 cups beef broth, low sodium
Bouquet Garni, recipe below
2 cups beer
Salt and pepper to taste

Bouquet Garni

1 sprig thyme
6 sprigs parsley
1 bay leaf
3 cloves

Chef's Tip

In keeping with the authenticity of the recipe and its heritage, use a good Belgian beer like Kesteel or Stella Artois, but get some extra—it's also great to drink!

Slice meat into 2 by ½-inch rectangles; season with salt and pepper. Tie the herbs of the bouquet garni together with twine. Spread mustard on bread. Preheat oven to 350°F. Heat oil and quickly brown meat over high heat; set aside. Melt butter in sauté pan, add onions, and cook until golden brown. Pour in vinegar and evaporate over high heat.

Alternate the layers of meat, carrots, and onions in an ovenproof 5-quart casserole, inserting the slice of bread and the bouquet garni in the middle. Pour the beer and raspberry preserves into a sauté pan and blend over high heat. Transfer to casserole, adding broth to cover meat. Cover and braise in oven for 4 hours without disturbing.

Transfer the meat and the carrots to a shallow dish and keep warm. Puree the bread, onions, and cooking juices through the fine holes of a food mill or a food processor to make a smooth sauce. Reheat the sauce over high heat, then pour over the meat. Serve immediately with mashed potatoes.

Courtesy Chef Nicolas Klontz, Zin American Bistro

BRAISED FREE-RANGE RABBIT WITH SPANISH ONIONS AND PEPPERS

Serves four

2 rabbits, free-range, cut into 8 pieces
2 Spanish onions, thinly sliced
3 cloves garlic
2 red peppers, roasted, peeled, seeded, and thinly sliced
2 yellow peppers, roasted, peeled, seeded, and thinly sliced
1 teaspoon smoked paprika
1 tablespoon tomato paste
½ cup flour
1 bouquet garni (thyme, 2 bay leaves, 4 cloves)
1 cup dry white wine
3 cups chicken broth
½ cup Spanish olive oil
Salt and black pepper to taste

Heat olive oil in a large skillet and brown the rabbit pieces in batches; season with salt and pepper and reserve. Add onions, garlic, and roasted peppers to the skillet and cook 10 minutes over medium heat, stirring frequently. Add smoked paprika, tomato paste, and flour and cook 3 minutes more, stirring frequently. Add rabbit pieces, bouquet garni, white wine, and chicken broth. Bring to a boil and simmer on low heat for 45 minutes until the rabbit is tender.

Courtesy of Chef Nicolas Klontz, Zin American Bistro

Chef's Tip

This is an excellent game dish; if you don't care for rabbit, try it with squab, pheasant, or quail.

VEAL SCALOPPINI WITH MUSHROOMS AND DRY WHITE VERMOUTH

Serves eight

8 veal scaloppini
¼ cup butter
3 tablespoons olive oil
1 clove garlic, minced
1 pound white button mushrooms
1 bunch fresh Italian flat-leaf parsley, chopped
½ cup white vermouth
2 tablespoons flour
Salt and pepper to taste

Clean and dry the mushrooms. Slice, but not too thinly. In a frying pan add the oil, a third of the butter and the garlic, and fry briefly. Add the mushrooms and cook briefly over high heat; add salt and pepper. Mushrooms should still be firm. Add half the parsley. Remove from heat and keep warm. Gently flatten the veal scaloppini, dust in flour, and remove excess. (If you are cooking the scaloppini in batches, do not flour them until you are ready to brown them. Do it too soon and the flour will get soggy and the veal will not brown properly.) Melt the remaining butter in a sauté pan and cook the veal over high heat about 1 minute each side. Do not overcook. Add the vermouth and let it evaporate, then add salt and pepper. Add the cooked mushrooms, and cook for 1 minute. Arrange on hot plates, garnish with remaining parsley, and serve.

Courtesy of Chef Vince Cultraro,
La Spiga Ristorante Italiano

Chef's Tip

This is not only a simple recipe, but it's one you can change easily. Use different mushrooms and you have a different result; use white wine rather than vermouth and again you change the flavors.

CHICKEN TANDOORI WITH SHRIMP AND MANGO

Serves four

This recipe calls for a tandoori paste and an 8-hour marinade time.

4 chicken breasts, 8 ounces each
4 tiger shrimp, 16/20 per pound-size
1 mango, peeled, sliced 1½ inches long, ½ inch thick
1 pinch of ground white pepper
1 pinch kosher salt
4 teaspoons olive oil
4 teaspoons garlic herb butter
4 servings basmati rice
Tandoori Paste, recipe follows

Place the chicken breasts smooth side down on a chopping board. With a small knife make a cut into each breast 1 inch deep and 2 inches long. Insert the whole shrimp and sliced mango into the cut.

Chef's Tip

Keep Tandoori stored in an airtight container in the freezer. It is also excellent on pork, as well as lamb and fish.

118

Tandoori Paste

1½ teaspoons ground ginger
½ teaspoon chili powder
1½ teaspoons ground coriander
1½ teaspoons paprika
1½ teaspoons tandoori powder
¾ cup natural yogurt
8 cloves garlic, roasted
¼ cup fresh lime juice
¼ cup minced cilantro

In a large bowl mix ginger, chili powder, coriander, paprika, and tandoori powder. Add the yogurt, garlic, and lime juice, then fold in the cilantro to create a paste. Set aside.

Place the chicken in the bowl with the tandoori paste. Cover it thoroughly with the marinade and refrigerate for at least 8 hours. In a medium sauté pan, heat the olive oil and butter, season the chicken with salt and pepper, and sear on both sides. Reduce the heat, cover, and then slowly cook for 4 minutes on each side, or until the chicken is fully cooked.

To Serve
Slice the chicken and present over basmati rice; garnish with fresh lime.

Courtesy of Chef Andrew Copley, Copley's on Palm Canyon

BIG-EYE TUNA TARTAR

¼ pound sushi-quality big-eye tuna, diced small
1 teaspoon chopped chives
1 teaspoon chopped cilantro
2 teaspoons toasted pine nuts
½ tablespoon chopped shallots
2-3 drops of lemon juice
1 teaspoon soy sauce
½ tablespoon extra-virgin olive oil
Salt and pepper to taste

In a mixing bowl, combine tuna, chives, cilantro, pine nuts, and shallots. Mix lightly; add salt, pepper, and olive oil; and mix again lightly. Just before serving, add lemon juice and soy sauce to taste. (Make sure the olive oil coats the tuna before adding the soy sauce and lemon juice; otherwise the acids will cook the fish as in a ceviche.)

Courtesy of Okura Robata
Grill & Sushi Bar

120

CRISPY FRIED SOFT-SHELL CRAB WITH SPICY SESAME MISO

1 piece soft-shell crab
1 tablespoon cornstarch

Spicy Sesame Miso, recipe below
Oil for frying

Preheat oil to 180°F, dust soft-shell crab in cornstarch, and deep-fry until crispy.

. . . .

Spicy Sesame Miso (large recipe)

¼ cup red miso
¼ cup white miso
3 tablespoons sugar
2 tablespoons mirin
1 tablespoon sake

3 tablespoons water
2 teaspoons Gochujang
  (Korean red chili sauce)
2 teaspoons white sesame seeds
1 teaspoon black sesame seeds

Combine all ingredients in a saucepan and cook over medium heat. Bring to a boil and simmer until set.

Courtesy of Okura Robata Grill & Sushi Bar

COLD POTATO-LEEK SOUP (VICHYSSOISE) • WATERMELON SOUP • SUMMER SALAD OF WATERCRESS • ERIC'S CAESAR SALAD SANDWICH • FAMOUS PEA AND NUT SALAD • BASIL ICE CREAM • TEQUILA DESERT SUNRISE JELLY

Cold Dishes

The Chill of Summer: Cold Dishes

IT HAS BEEN ONE OF THOSE LATE JULY DAYS that hit 110°F and you realize that August is still to come and that September will give you no guarantee of cooler weather. Until just a few years ago, the desert cities would have been nearly deserted and all the restaurants closed for the summer. That has changed; there are more and more year-round residents and some of the best restaurants are staying open for the season, with perhaps a couple of weeks' vacation in August, when the spirit flags.

I was in a restaurant outlining the plans for this book to two friends, who were also eating there. They are both very good cooks and have established a reputation for the perfectionism of their dinner parties: they take food very seriously indeed. They looked at me quizzically and said, "Aren't you going to have a chapter on menus when the weather is like this?" And of course they were right. Diehard desert dwellers don't give up entertaining just because the temperature is threatening to reach 115°F or even 120°F. They stay inside and plan.

I knew this perfectly well but somehow the knowledge hadn't made its way into my initial outline. I hastily added another chapter heading and asked Michael and Steven to let me have some of their recipes. Then I went on a hunt for recipes particularly appropriate for our hottest evenings—every chef or home cook had some.

COLD POTATO-LEEK SOUP (VICHYSSOISE)

Serves six

4 leeks, cut in half and washed
¾ cup shallots, chopped ¼ inch thick
⅔ cup onions, sliced ¼ inch thick
½ pound russet potatoes, peeled, chopped
1 tablespoon garlic, minced
1 sachet (6–7 inches of dark green leek leaves, 8 thyme sprigs, 2 Italian parsley
** sprigs, 2 bay leaves, and 8 black peppercorns)**
6 cups chicken stock
1 cup heavy cream
½ cup chives, minced
2 tablespoons extra-virgin olive oil or white truffle oil
Kosher salt and black pepper to taste

Using only the white and pale green parts of the leeks, cut lengthwise in half and rinse. Cut into ¼-inch slices. Melt butter in a large saucepan; then add the leeks, onions, and shallots; and season with kosher salt and pepper. Sweat the vegetables for 4–5 minutes until wilted but not brown.

Cut the potato into ¼-inch slices. Add garlic to the cooking vegetables and cook for about 1 minute, then add the potato and cook for another 2–4 minutes. Then add 5½ cups of the chicken stock and the sachet and season to taste. Reduce heat and simmer for 30 minutes. When the potatoes are tender, remove from heat and let cool at least 10 minutes.

Remove the sachet and prepare an ice bath if you are going to refrigerate the soup. This day-ahead method is recommended, as it lets the soup come into its own and lessens the work on the day of the dinner party. Transfer the soup in batches to a blender and puree at low speed, then on high until smooth. Strain the soup through a fine-mesh sieve twice, which guarantees a fine, smooth texture. Refrigerate. When preparing to serve, return soup to pan, add the cream, and simmer for 5 minutes. Place the soup in a container and refrigerate. Serve each portion with a bit of the chopped chives and a swirl of oil.

Courtesy of Michael Huard and Steven Winkler

Chef's Tip

Increase the ratio of shallot and onion to potato in this recipe for the most flavor.

WATERMELON SOUP

Serves six

1 seedless watermelon, rind removed, chopped
3 limes
1 jalapeño pepper, seeded and minced
1 small ring of habanero pepper
1 teaspoon minced fresh ginger

Zest and juice 2 limes, add to a blender, then add in the watermelon, jalapeño, habanero, and ginger. Puree in a blender until smooth. Then strain through a sieve. Refrigerate until completely cold. Serve in a bowl with wedges of lime.

Courtesy of Citron Restaurant,
the Viceroy Hotel

SUMMER SALAD OF WATERCRESS

Serves four

3 bunches watercress
½ lemon, sliced, for garnish
Kosher salt and freshly ground black pepper to taste
Vinaigrette, recipe below

Vinaigrette

⅓ cup sherry vinegar, fine quality
½ cup extra-virgin olive oil, fine quality
2 tablespoons fresh lemon juice
2 teaspoons shallot, minced

Pour the sherry vinegar into a bowl and add the shallot and lemon juice. Using a small whisk, drizzle in the olive oil until well mixed. Season to taste and also to balance the ingredients. Set aside and let rest for about 2 hours. Strain the dressing, removing the shallot and keeping the essence; season again to taste. The vinaigrette should be simple with a slightly citrus quality.

TO FINISH

Wash and stem all of the watercress; this important step will make the salad pleasant in texture to the mouth and is worth the effort. Toss the watercress with just enough dressing to very lightly coat; do not overdress. To present, place a 3-inch ring mold in the center of a large plate, fill with the watercress, remove the mold, and place a small lemon slice to the side.

Courtesy of Michael Huard and Steven Winkler

Chef's Tip

Try using a 25-year aged sherry vinegar for this recipe; it will add a deeper, slightly sweet flavor that will go beautifully with the peppery watercress.

HUARD AND WINKLER SERVE THEIR WATERCRESS SALAD traditionally after the entrée. The following salads, however, would probably be used more suitably as appetizers or even as light lunches or buffet side dishes.

ERIC'S CAESAR SALAD SANDWICH

Serves four

3 romaine hearts, cut to 5-inch length, washed and dried
1 cup Parmigiano-Reggiano cheese, grated small
1 cup Lemony Caesar Dressing, recipe follows
1 sourdough bread loaf
¼ cup olive oil
Sea salt and freshly ground black pepper to taste

Slice the sourdough loaf crosswise, ⅛ inch thick. Place 8 slices on jelly roll pans and brush with olive oil, then sprinkle with the grated cheese, salt, and pepper. Bake in a 350°F oven for 10 minutes, remove, and let cool. In large mixing bowl toss the romaine with the Lemony Caesar dressing, salt, and pepper. Place one sourdough crisp on a plate and then arrange the romaine leaves on the crisp, top with another piece of sourdough crisp. Repeat the procedure 3 times.

Continued on next page

Chef's Tip

When making this or any other salad, use an extra-large mixing bowl, as this will help to prevent bruising the lettuce.

127

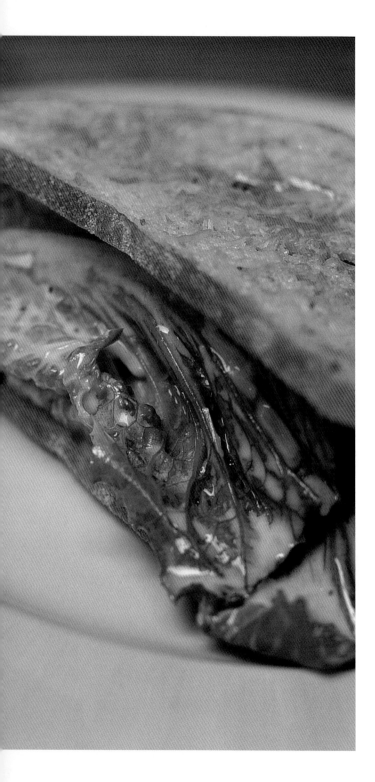

Lemony Caesar Dressing

6 egg yolks
2 tablespoons Dijon mustard
3 tablespoons garlic, minced
2 anchovies
3 cups extra-virgin olive oil
¾ cup champagne vinegar
4 tablespoons lemon juice
1 teaspoon Tabasco sauce
1 tablespoon Worcestershire sauce
Sea salt and freshly ground black pepper to taste

In a food processor, add the egg yolks. Mix until creamy and then add the Dijon, garlic, and anchovies. Slowly incorporate half the oil, then add half the lemon juice. Add the remaining oil followed by the lemon juice. Add all of the remaining ingredients. Season the dressing with salt and pepper to taste, and keep refrigerated.

Courtesy of Chef Eric Wadlund, Beefsteak Restaurant

MAURICE BRATT IS A RESTAURANT CRITIC and food writer who hosts the radio food talk show *Dishing with Maurice,* heard on Saturdays from noon until 2 p.m. on KGAM 1450 AM. Before he took to the airwaves he ran a successful catering business in the desert.

FAMOUS PEA AND NUT SALAD

Serves four

1 10-ounce package petite peas, frozen
1 cup celery, diced
1 cup cashews, unsalted
¼ cup scallion, thinly sliced
¼ cup bacon, cooked and minced
¼ cup French or Italian dressing
Salt and freshly ground black pepper to taste
1 cup sour cream or yogurt
8 bibb lettuce leaves, cold and crisp

Thaw out the peas and rinse with cold water in a colander. In a large mixing bowl, add all of the salad ingredients except the lettuce, then the dressing and yogurt. Fold the salad together gently so as not to smash the peas, season with salt and pepper, and chill. To serve, place small amounts of the salad in the bibb lettuce cups and arrange them on a platter.

Courtesy of Maurice Bratt

Chef's Tip

You can prepare the salad the day before you need it; keep it in the refrigerator in an airtight container.

BASIL ICE CREAM

Makes three pints

3 cups fresh basil leaves, packed
¼ cup simple syrup
1½ cups whole milk
3 cups heavy cream
1½ cups sugar
12 egg yolks
1 vanilla bean
1 pinch of salt

Blanch the basil in boiling water, refresh in ice water, then drain the leaves and puree in a blender with simple syrup. Combine the milk, cream, ¾ cup of sugar, and vanilla bean, then bring the mixture to a simmer. Whisk together the egg yolks and remaining sugar. Remove the milk mixture from the heat and, whisking constantly, add the egg yolks. Return to the stove and cook over low heat until it thickens to coat the back of a wooden spoon. Cover and refrigerate for 4 hours. Add the basil puree to the base mixture and mix in an electric ice cream maker for 35 minutes.

Courtesy Copley's on Palm Canyon

Chef's Tip

There are two kinds of ice cream, cooked and uncooked. This recipe is the cooked kind; it will give you a richer ice cream with more body.

THE ONLY THING THAT CAN MATCH ICE CREAM for a hot summer night's last course is an English jelly. Nowadays gelatin has become a very trendy item in the avant garde chef's repertoire, but an English jelly isn't avant garde at all. With the right ingredients it can be sophisticated, though. In America the mixture of alcohol and gelatin reminds people of Jell-O shots and their college days, but a jelly made with the proportions of a good cocktail is a pudding fit for grown-ups. The first sensation is mouth feel: cool, smooth, bland; then the flavor bursts through.

One slight problem: there seems to be no current word in America for this sort of pudding; "jelly" means something else and the brand name Jell-O has taken over in general usage. "If it doesn't jell it isn't aspic," said the detective in Hitchcock's *Psycho*. In Gus Van Sant's remake he said, "It isn't Jell-O." So obviously the word "aspic" is archaic. Professional chefs sometimes use the word "gelée," but that sounds insufferably pretentious in any ordinary house. You'll have to make up your own mind what to call this dish, but whatever you call it, it's good. Being English, I'll stick with calling it "jelly."

TEQUILA DESERT SUNRISE JELLY

Makes one four-cup mold

2 cups orange juice, freshly squeezed
1 cup sugar
1¼ cups tequila
½ cup grenadine

3 envelopes unflavored gelatin
1 orange, zest only
1 cup water
¾ cup cold water

Make syrup by combining 1 cup of the water and ½ cup orange juice in a saucepan with 1 cup sugar. Bring to a boil and simmer for 5 minutes. Remove from heat and add orange zest. Steep for 15 minutes, then strain into a measuring cup. This should produce about 1¼ cups of syrup. Add the rest of the orange juice to make about 2¾ cups liquid total. Add enough tequila to make 4 cups of liquid total.

Empty the envelopes of unflavored gelatin into a small saucepan along with ¾ cup cold water. Leave for 5 minutes to absorb water, then heat on low and stir until completely dissolved, about 1 minute.

Continued on next page

Chef's Tip

Remember that the alcohol isn't dissipated in this mode of preparation.

131

Stir in some of the tequila-orange mixture, making sure that the gelatin is completely dissolved. Add about a sixth of the gelatin mix to the grenadine and then stir. Add the remainder of the gelatin mix to the tequila-orange mixture and stir. Pour the tequila-orange gelée mixture into molds, leaving a small portion at the top of the mold for the grenadine to be added later. Let cool. Keep the grenadine gelée mixture aside while it also cools.

When cool, refrigerate for about 1 hour, then remove and add grenadine mixture to the top of the molds. (If you want the red and orange to mix, add the grenadine earlier.) Return to the refrigerator and chill for 5 hours or until set. Dip the molds very quickly into hot water and unmold the jellies onto plates. The grenadine layer, which was on the top of the mold, will now be on the bottom. Decorate the jellies with raspberries and orange slices and serve.

Courtesy of Henry Fenwick

TEQUILA, LIME, AND GARLIC FLANK STEAK SALAD • SHRIMP SALAD WITH WHITE BEANS, ARTICHOKE HEARTS, AND ORANGE-MINT DRESSING • MEDITERRANEAN ROASTED PEPPER, OLIVE, AND TOMATO RELISH • CITRUS SHRIMP SKEWERS • GINGER-SOY PORK TENDERLOINS • GUACAMOLE DEVILED EGGS • HOISIN LAMB CHOPS • CAPONATA • ARTICHOKE CAVIAR IN BOSTON LETTUCE CUPS • GRILLED ASPARAGUS WITH YELLOW AND RED PEPPER SALSA • STANDING RIB ROAST WITH CILANTRO-GARLIC SAUCE AND GRILLED SWEET POTATOES

Catering Dishes

Partying for the Greater Good

THOUGH MORE AND MORE PEOPLE ARE NOW LIVING IN THE DESERT year-round, there is still a definite season, and that season is a very social one. It's approximately a six-month affair; it begins as the temperatures start to fall in October and November, revs up with the New Year, then reaches its peak in February and March. By April it's getting quiet and come May it's almost over. While the season is in full flood, it's marked by benefits, auctions, galas, and balls, how, when, and wherever people can gather together and party for a good cause.

Benefits and fundraisers can operate on any level, from a small brunch for a group of alumni who are raising funds for scholarships to blockbusters collecting the necessary financial backing for museums and arts festivals. The first event of the season, Dinner in the Canyons, is held in October to benefit the Agua Caliente Indians Museum. Since it's literally in the canyons, it can't be too formal, but since it's for Indian affairs, all the politicians show up, which means it can't be completely casual. The black ties start to come out in November. December grants a family holiday hiatus but January has both major golf and major film events, including the Bob Hope Classic golf tournament (and parties) and the Palm Springs International Film Festival (and parties). Film people who like golf are in for a heavy month.

And the beat goes on. Which means, of course, that there is a continual demand for the services of caterers. Indeed, the desert is famous, perhaps notorious, for luxurious homes with state-of-the-art kitchens that get used only when the professionals move in. We went to some of those professionals to garner recipes that make for successful party-giving.

135

TEQUILA, LIME, AND GARLIC FLANK STEAK SALAD

Serves six

1 flank steak, about 3 pounds
1 cup Tequila, Lime and Garlic Marinade, recipe below
½ cup slivered red onion
½ cup slivered red bell pepper
½ cup slivered yellow bell pepper
¼ cup cilantro, chopped
1 tablespoon chili powder
2 tablespoons honey
¼ cup lime juice, fresh
1 tablespoon garlic, minced
Salt and pepper to taste

Pierce steak with a fork. Mix all the marinade ingredients together, pour over steaks and marinate for at least 3 hours, preferably overnight. Heat a gas or charcoal grill and grill steak to desired doneness, turning frequently. Let meat rest for at least 15 minutes, then slice across the grain into thin strips. Mix well with rest of ingredients and serve.

• • • • • • • • • • • • •

Tequila, Lime, and Garlic Marinade

⅓ cup fresh lime juice
⅓ cup olive oil
¼ cup soy sauce
¼ cup tequila
3 tablespoons garlic, minced
1 tablespoon cumin
1 tablespoon oregano
Salt and pepper to taste

In a large bowl combine all ingredients and mix well.

Courtesy of Chef Jennifer Johnson,
Jennifer's Kitchen

Chef's Tip

Since flank steak is not a very expensive cut of meat, if the party budget allows it you might consider upgrading to certified Angus or even USDA Prime.

SHRIMP SALAD WITH WHITE BEANS, ARTICHOKE HEARTS, AND ORANGE-MINT DRESSING

Serves ten

2½ pounds large shrimp, peeled, deveined, tails removed
2 tablespoons olive oil
2 tablespoons butter, unsalted
1 tablespoon minced garlic
2 cups artichoke chopped hearts
6 cups white beans, cooked
1 cup slivered red onion
½ cup slivered yellow peppers
½ cup slivered red peppers
¾ cup Orange-Mint Dressing, recipe below
Salt and pepper to taste
½ cup fresh mint, julienne, for garnish

In a large sauté pan, heat oil and butter; when hot, add garlic and shrimp and sauté until shrimp is cooked through. Let cool. In large bowl combine rest of the ingredients, toss with dressing, top with shrimp, and garnish with fresh mint.

Orange-Mint Dressing

3 tablespoons Dijon mustard
3 tablespoons honey
⅓ cup orange juice, fresh squeezed
3 tablespoons sherry vinegar
¾ cup olive oil
1 tablespoon orange zest
⅓ cup fresh mint, chopped
Salt and pepper to taste

In a large bowl, blend mustard, honey, orange juice, and vinegar; slowly whisk in olive oil to emulsify. Add zest, mint, and salt and pepper to blend.

Courtesy of Chef Jennifer Johnson, Jennifer's Kitchen

Chef's Tip

When buying shrimp, always buy white shrimp rather than tiger; the white shrimp are more tender.

137

MEDITERRANEAN ROASTED PEPPER, OLIVE, AND TOMATO RELISH

Serves six

2 orange bell peppers
2 yellow bell peppers
2 red bell peppers
4 large tomatoes
1 tablespoon chopped garlic
1 cup fresh basil, parsley, and sage, chopped
2 tablespoons capers
⅓ cup chopped Kalamata olives
⅓ cup olive oil
1½ tablespoons balsamic vinegar
Kosher salt and black pepper to taste

Chef's Tip

As an hors d'oeuvre this is great with goat cheese or feta cheese and crusty bread; it is also fabulous as a topping on grilled fish or chicken.

Grill or roast the peppers until charred. Let cool. Peel, seed, and cut into julienne strips. Score the ends of tomatoes, drop into boiling water for 15 seconds, remove and place in an ice bath. Then remove the skins, cut in half, remove seeds, and cut into strips about the same size as the peppers. Toss peppers and tomatoes with the rest of the ingredients and bake at 375°F for 25 minutes. Let cool. Season with kosher salt and pepper.

*Courtesy of
Chef Jennifer Johnson,
Jennifer's Kitchen*

CITRUS SHRIMP SKEWERS

Serves four

12 shrimp, 16–20 per pound-size
1 tablespoon Old Bay seasoning
2 pinches of sea salt
1 teaspoon minced garlic
1 tablespoon fresh parsley, minced
1 teaspoon orange zest
1 tablespoon butter, unsalted
12 bamboo skewers

Clean and devein shrimp, keeping the tail on. Run each bamboo skewer from the tail end through the shrimp. Place a sauté pan over medium heat and add butter to melt. Place shrimp in butter, sprinkle with Old Bay Seasoning, and cook until pink on both sides. Add garlic, parsley, and orange zest, and cook 2 more minutes, being careful not to overcook, as the garlic will become bitter. Let them cool and then skewer the shrimp in a half of an orange for a dramatic yet simple display.

Courtesy of Sherry Peña, Desert Cities Catering

Chef's Tip

When buying your shrimp, ask that the fishmonger clean them for you. They're often happy to do it.

GINGER-SOY PORK TENDERLOINS

Serves four

4 pork tenderloins, 7 ounces each	**1 tablespoon fresh ginger, grated**
½ cup olive oil	**1 tablespoon fresh garlic, minced**
½ cup soy sauce	**2 pinches of sea salt**

Mix marinade ingredients together and marinate the tenderloins in a zip-top bag for at least 2 hours. Grill for 15–20 minutes. Let stand for 5 minutes, then slice.

Courtesy of Sherry Peña, Desert Cities Catering

GUACAMOLE DEVILED EGGS

Serves four

6 hard-boiled eggs
2 avocados
1 tablespoon red onion, minced
1 tablespoon jalapeño, minced
1 clove garlic, minced
3 dashes of Tabasco sauce
12 cilantro leaves
Sea salt to taste

Cut eggs in half, remove yolk, place in a small bowl, and mash. Smash the avocado and then add the mashed yolks, onion, jalapeño, garlic, salt, and Tabasco. Put guacamole in a pastry bag and pipe, or spoon into the egg halves. Garnish with the cilantro.

Courtesy of Sherry Peña,
Desert Cities Catering

HOISIN LAMB CHOPS

Serves four

3 racks of lamb, about 14 ounces each
2¼ cups hoisin sauce
1 clove garlic, minced
Sea salt to taste

Rub lamb with garlic, salt, and hoisin sauce. Charbroil for 15–20 minutes.

Courtesy of Sherry Peña, Desert Cities Catering

Chef's Tip

When buying lamb, ask the butcher for American lamb; it is less gamey and more tender than the New Zealand lamb.

THELMA PRESSMAN PIONEERED microwave cooking, is the author of several books on the subject, and was a regular columnist for *Bon Appétit* magazine. Thelma also ran a cooking school in Encino, California, before moving to the desert.

CAPONATA

Makes four cups

Try this time-saving microwave method for a classic dish.

1 large eggplant	½ cup coarsely chopped black olives
½ cup extra-virgin olive oil	⅓ cup red wine vinegar
1 cup coarsely chopped onion	2 tablespoons sugar
1 cup coarsely chopped celery	1 tablespoon capers
1 cup chopped red bell pepper	1½ teaspoons salt
1 cup tomato sauce	½ teaspoon pepper

Cut unpeeled eggplant into ½-inch cubes. Pour oil into a 2-quart casserole, cover with a lid, and heat in microwave on high for 1½ minutes. Stir in the eggplant, cover again, and cook on high 10 minutes, stirring twice. Stir in onion, celery, and red pepper. Cover and cook on high for 2 minutes. Stir in the tomato sauce, olives, vinegar, sugar, capers, salt, and pepper. Cook, uncovered, for 10 minutes, stirring twice. Serve at room temperature or cover and refrigerate until chilled. The flavor improves on standing.

Courtesy of Thelma Pressman

Chef's Tip

Caponata was originally a Sicilian dish of eggplant, pine nuts, and other vegetables—usually a vegetable dish, though anchovies or anchovy sauce may be added. It is cooked in olive oil and served at room temperature, often as an appetizer. Every town and village in Sicily has its own version, eggplant being the constant.

UNTIL RECENTLY, GOURMET COOKING IN THE DESERT would've been nearly impossible without Jensen's Finest Foods. Their first market opened in 1940, and there are now nine branches throughout the area. With the growth of the desert cities, other sources for gourmet ingredients are opening up, but Jensen's remains a desert bulwark.

ARTICHOKE CAVIAR IN BOSTON LETTUCE CUPS

Serves four

2 cups marinated artichoke hearts
½ cup diced small zucchini
2 tablespoons diced small green onion
1 tomato, seeded, diced small
1 teaspoon lemon juice
2 cloves minced garlic
Salt and pepper to taste
12 small Boston lettuce cups

Drain the artichoke hearts, reserving about ⅓ cup of the marinade; set aside. Cut the artichokes to a small dice. In a mixing bowl add the artichokes, zucchini, onion, tomato, garlic, lemon juice, and the reserved marinade. Mix well and then season with salt and pepper. Refrigerate for 4 hours. To serve, place a tablespoon of the artichoke caviar into the Boston lettuce cups.

Courtesy of Jensen's Finest Foods

GRILLED ASPARAGUS WITH YELLOW AND RED PEPPER SALSA

3 pounds asparagus, trimmed
¼ cup olive oil
Salt and pepper to taste
1 cup Yellow and Red Pepper Salsa, recipe below

Yellow and Red Pepper Salsa

1 red pepper, seeded, diced
1 yellow pepper, seeded, diced
½ red onion
2 tablespoons lime juice
2 tablespoons jalapeño jelly
2 tablespoons vegetable oil
1 jalapeño, seeded and minced
2 tablespoons chopped cilantro
Salt and pepper to taste

In a large mixing bowl combine all ingredients and mix well; season with salt and pepper.

TO FINISH

Light the grill and heat to medium. While the grill is warming, lightly coat the asparagus with olive oil and season with salt and pepper. Grill the asparagus until it is tender and begins to brown, turning frequently, for about 5 minutes. Transfer the asparagus to a platter and top with the salsa. Serve warm.

Courtesy of Jensen's Finest Foods

STANDING RIB ROAST WITH CILANTRO-GARLIC SAUCE AND GRILLED SWEET POTATOES

Serves six

This recipe requires preparing a cilantro-garlic sauce and grilled sweet potatoes.

1 standing beef rib roast, 3 pounds
3 cloves garlic, sliced thin
3 tablespoons Dijon mustard
Salt and pepper to taste
1 cup Cilantro-Garlic Sauce, recipe below
4 cups Grilled Sweet Potatoes, recipe follows

. . . .

Cilantro-Garlic Sauce

1 bunch cilantro, washed, stemmed, and chopped
8 cloves chopped garlic
3 tablespoons minced onion
5 tablespoons red wine vinegar
5 tablespoons water
1 teaspoon hot pepper flakes
1 cup extra-virgin olive oil
Salt and pepper to taste

In a food processor add the cilantro, garlic, onion, vinegar, water, and pepper flakes and process in brief bursts. Once smooth, slowly add the olive oil and season with salt and pepper.

Chef's Tip

When it is time to entertain, one of my favorite dishes to make is prime rib. This is also a fantastic time to open a bottle of red wine. When cooking large pieces of beef, remember to allow about 20 minutes of cooking-time per pound.

Grilled Sweet Potatoes

2 pounds sweet potatoes, peeled
  and cut into eighths
½ cup olive oil
1½ tablespoons fresh thyme, chopped
1 red onion, cut into wedges
1 red pepper, seeded, cut into eighths
2 tablespoons apple cider vinegar
Salt and pepper to taste

Light the grill and heat to medium. While
the grill is warming up, lightly coat the
potatoes, pepper, and onion with ¼ cup
of the oil, thyme, salt, and pepper. Grill
the vegetables until tender, turning often,
15–20 minutes. Transfer the vegetables to a
platter. In a mixing bowl add the remaining
ingredients, whisk together the remaining
oil and vinegar, season with salt and pepper,
then drizzle over the vegetables.

To Finish
Make small slits in the beef rib roast with
the tip of a paring knife and insert the garlic
slivers. Rub the beef with the mustard and
season generously with salt and pepper.
Place the beef in a shallow roasting pan
and roast at 450°F for 25 minutes, then
reduce the heat to 350°F and let cook
for another 30 minutes, or until the roast
reaches an internal temperature of 135°F
for medium doneness. Remove the roast
from the oven and let it rest for 10–15
minutes before carving.

Courtesy of Jensen's Finest Foods

COFFEE AND DONUTS • DEEP-DISH BROWNIE • BANANA SPLIT • CHOCOLATE CHUNK PIE • STRAWBERRY-RHUBARB CRISP • BANANA TART • PASSION FRUIT PANNA COTTA WITH BLUEBERRY SAUCE • CHOCOLATE-CHOCOLATE CAKE WITH RASPBERRIES & VANILLA BEAN ICE CREAM • CHOCOLATE-CAPPUCCINO MOUSSE CAKE • BAKED THIN APPLE TART • DESERT BREAD PUDDING • SWEET CREPES WITH VANILLA-SAUTÉED STRAWBERRIES • LA QUINTA LEMON BARS

Dessert

Last Course: Dessert

DESERT SNOWBIRDS (those part-time refugees from colder climates in Chicago, Toronto, Seattle, New York, and other wintry cities) often spend almost half their year in the warmth of the Palm Springs area, and when they're in town, they like to go out to eat. They don't skimp on desserts—indeed, their taste is lavish and comfort loving. Full-time desert residents follow their example—old-fashioned nursery puddings or chic versions of the same are the most popular desserts of all.

A case in point is Arnold Palmer's Restaurant, in La Quinta. Arnold Palmer is a much-loved desert figure, and his restaurant is popular with everyone who golfs—which accounts for a large proportion of desert visitors and residents—and with a lot of those who don't. The menu features Arnie's own favorite dishes, which are simple, old-fashioned, and filling. The desserts are famous for following in the same tradition.

COFFEE AND DONUTS

Serves eight

1 extra-large egg	½ cup milk
½ cup sugar	1⅓ cups flour
¾ tablespoon baking powder	½ cup sugar
¼ teaspoon salt	⅓ tablespoon cinnamon
1 teaspoon clarified butter	1 quart coffee ice cream
½ teaspoon ground nutmeg	1 cup whipped cream
½ teaspoon powdered ginger	

With a mixer, beat the eggs until thick and lemon-colored. Then add the sugar, baking powder, salt, clarified butter, nutmeg, ginger, milk, and flour and mix until it reaches dough consistency. On a breadboard dusted with flour and ginger, roll a ½-ounce ball. Using this as a guide, roll the remaining donut holes.

Place the donut holes on a sheet pan lined with parchment paper. Cover with a clean kitchen towel and let stand for 1 hour. Prepare a brown paper bag with ½ cup of sugar and 1 tablespoon of cinnamon. Deep-fry the donut holes at 300°F until golden brown. Place the donut holes in the brown paper bag and shake to coat with the seasoned sugar.

To Finish
For each serving, use a coffee cup and saucer. Place 4 donut holes on the saucer, fill the cup with ice cream, and top with whipped cream.

Courtesy of Arnold Palmer's Restaurant

150

DEEP-DISH BROWNIE

¾ **pound cubed butter**
¾ **pound granulated sugar**
¾ **pound semisweet chocolate, cut in ½-inch cubes**
¼ **cup flour**
1⅓ **cups egg whites**
½ **cup pasteurized egg yolks**
2 **cups chocolate fudge sauce**
¾ **quart vanilla ice cream**

Fill a saucepan with 3 inches of water and bring to a simmer. In a medium stainless-steel bowl, melt the butter, sugar, and chocolate together over the saucepan, stirring occasionally. When the ingredients have melted, sift in the flour and stir to combine. Let the mixture cool to room temperature.

With a mixer, bring the egg yolks to ribbons and set aside. With a mixer, bring the egg whites to stiff peaks. Then add the egg yolks to the chocolate mixture and thoroughly combine. Using a plastic spatula, carefully fold in the egg whites to capture the air. Spray the inside of a straight-sided bowl and coat with flour. Fill each bowl with ¾ cup of brownie mix. In a 325° oven, place the bowls on a sheet pan and bake for 40 minutes. Allow brownie to cool completely before placing in refrigerator. To serve, place brownie in 300° oven for 8 minutes. Top warm brownie with a scoop of vanilla ice cream and top with chocolate fudge sauce.

Courtesy of Arnold Palmer's Restaurant

Chef's Tip

The brownies for this recipe should be made one to two days in advance of serving.

151

Dessert

PENNSYLVANIA CLAIMS THE BANANA SPLIT as its creation (Ohio challenges that) and Arnold Palmer comes from Pennsylvania. Naturally, a banana split is an important item on his dessert menu—a Pennsylvania banana split.

BANANA SPLIT

Serves six

6 bananas, sliced in half lengthwise
1 quart vanilla ice cream
1 quart strawberry ice cream
1 quart chocolate ice cream
1 full cup chocolate sauce
1 full cup strawberry sauce
1 can whipped cream
18 maraschino cherries
12 tablespoons crushed pineapple
12 tablespoons chopped walnuts

Place one split banana in each dessert dish. Add one scoop of each ice cream flavor between the bananas. Drizzle the chocolate and strawberry sauce over the ice cream. Decorate each scoop of ice cream with the whipped cream. Place a maraschino cherry on each of the scoops. Sprinkle one heaping tablespoon of crushed pineapple and chopped walnuts down the length of the split.

Courtesy of Arnold Palmer's Restaurant

CHOCOLATE CHUNK PIE

Makes one pie

1 prepared pie crust, 9-inch
¾ cup flour
¾ cup granulated sugar
¾ cup brown sugar
½ pound butter, unsalted,
   cut in 1-inch cubes
2 extra-large eggs

½ cup semisweet chocolate chips
½ cup semisweet vanilla chips
¾ cup candied walnuts
½ teaspoon vanilla
1 quart vanilla ice cream
½ cup chocolate syrup
4 tablespoons powdered sugar

Add the granulated sugar, brown sugar, and butter to a mixing bowl and blend on medium speed. Add the eggs, flour, and vanilla and then continue mixing until it reaches a cookie dough consistency. Remove the mixing bowl and fold the chocolate and vanilla chips into the dough.

Preheat oven to 325°F. Fill the pie shell with cookie dough. Bake on the bottom rack until golden brown. When the pie is done, place it, uncovered, on a ventilated rack and bring to room temperature.

TO FINISH
Place one slice on each plate, add one scoop of vanilla ice cream, sprinkle with powdered sugar and walnuts and then drizzle with one tablespoon of chocolate syrup.

Courtesy of Arnold Palmer's Restaurant

ONLY A SHORT DISTANCE AWAY FROM ARNOLD PALMER'S IN MILES, but a long way away in style, is the restaurant Blend. There, Chef Kevin Kathman and his wife, pastry chef Kori Jacobson, have made an impact with a cuisine that reflects Kathman's background working for such Michelin three-star chefs as Thomas Keller and Gordon Ramsay. Kori's desserts will leave you relaxed, happy, and savoring the flavors you have enjoyed.

STRAWBERRY-RHUBARB CRISP

Serves six

3 cups finely chopped strawberries
3 cups finely chopped rhubarb
1 cup sugar
3 tablespoons cornstarch
1 tablespoon fresh ginger, grated fine
1 teaspoon salt
Juice of 1 lemon
2 cups Crumb Topping, recipe follows
Vanilla ice cream for topping

Mix all ingredients in a medium bowl; let stand for 10 minutes. Place in baking dish and evenly distribute all the juices. Bake 10 minutes at 350°. Add crumb topping and bake for another 10 minutes. Remove the crisp from the oven and let cool for 5–10 minutes. Top with vanilla ice cream.

Crumb Topping

1 cup flour
1 cup brown sugar
1 cup butter
1 cup sliced almonds
1 cup pecan pieces

Mix flour and sugar together. Blend in butter until mixture forms into pea-sized crumbles. Add nuts.

Courtesy of Chef Kori Jacobson, Blend Restaurant

Dessert

BANANA TART

Serves two

2 tart shells
2 cups caramel sauce
1 banana

1 cup Banana Mousse, recipe below
¼ cup sugar

• •

Banana Mousse

1 banana
4 cups heavy cream
Juice of 1 lemon

Blend banana and 1 cup heavy cream. Add to mixing bowl with remaining ingredients and blend until stiff peaks form.

TO SERVE
Pour the caramel sauce into the tart shells, follow with banana mousse, add sliced banana and sugar, then caramelize the sugar with a blowtorch.

Courtesy of Chef Kori Jacobson,
Blend Restaurant

PASSION FRUIT PANNA COTTA WITH BLUEBERRY SAUCE

Panna Cotta

⅓ cup sugar
1¾ cups heavy cream
¼ cup whole milk
½ cup pureed passion fruit
3 sheets gelatin
2 cups Blueberry Sauce, recipe below

Blueberry Sauce

1 cup blueberries (fresh if available, otherwise frozen)
1 cup water
¼ cup sugar
Juice of ½ lemon

Place ingredients in small saucepot and bring to a boil. Strain through a fine sieve. Return to heat and simmer until reduced by half, then chill.

TO FINISH

In a heavy saucepan add cream, sugar, milk, and puree. Over medium-high heat bring mixture almost to a boil. Bloom the gelatin in cold water, ring out the gelatin, and add it to the hot cream liquid. Cool the panna cotta mixture down in a water bath, then pour into 5-ounce molds. Refrigerate for 6 hours and then unmold. Serve topped with the blueberry sauce.

Courtesy of Chef Kori Jacobson, Blend Restaurant

Chef's Tip

Gelatin sheets can be found on the Internet. They work differently from powder and are worth the effort to find and use.

Dessert

NO RESTAURANT IN THE VALLEY CAN AFFORD TO IGNORE DESSERTS, and chocolate is always a crowd pleaser. David Nelson, the La Quinta pastry chef, pleases crowds continually.

CHOCOLATE-CHOCOLATE CAKE WITH RASPBERRIES & VANILLA BEAN ICE CREAM

Makes one cake

½ cup plus 1 tablespoon cake flour
2 cups sugar
3 tablespoons cocoa powder
1 tablespoon baking powder
1 pinch of baking soda
5 eggs

½ cup liquid shortening
¼ cup plus 1 tablespoon buttermilk
2 pints raspberries
1 quart vanilla bean ice cream
Chocolate Ganache, recipe below

In a large mixing bowl combine the flour, sugar, cocoa powder, baking powder, baking soda, and eggs; whip these ingredients on high speed for 8 minutes. Add the liquid shortening and whip for an additional 8 minutes, then incorporate the buttermilk on slow speed until thoroughly combined. Butter and flour a 10-inch cake pan. Pour the batter into the pan and bake at 350°F for 40 minutes. Remove from oven and place on a cooling rack.

· ·

Chocolate Ganache

1 pound heavy cream
2 pounds Belgian chocolate, broken into chunks

Place a heavy-bottomed saucepan over high heat. Bring the heavy cream to a boil, remove from heat, and add the chocolate, letting it "melt in" for one minute. Stir until smooth and well incorporated.

When preparing to make this cake, spend a little money and buy a high-quality chocolate such as Valrhona or Callebout.

158

To Assemble the Cake

Slice the domed top off of the cake and save it for some other use, then slice the cake horizontally 3 times. Place the first layer in a 10-inch cake pan and ladle in 2 cups of the ganache, then place the second layer of cake and another 2 cups of ganache. Top with the last piece of cake, then chill for 4–6 hours. When the cake is firm, cut into 10 to 12 pieces. Stand a wedge of the cake on end and drizzle with ¼ cup of ganache. Garnish with raspberries and vanilla bean ice cream.

Courtesy Chef David Nelson, La Quinta Resort & Club

CHOCOLATE-CAPPUCCINO MOUSSE CAKE

Makes one 12-inch cake

¼ cup plus 2 tablespoons bittersweet chocolate
3 tablespoons almond meal (raw, blanched almonds ground into a fine powder)
3 tablespoons flour
3 eggs
¼ cup plus 1 tablespoon granulated sugar
Mousse, recipe below

Cream eggs and sugar until white and fluffy. Mix together melted chocolate and butter. Incorporate chocolate mixture, flour, and almond meal into the egg and sugar mixture. Pour into a 12-inch form and bake at 325°F for 15 minutes.

Mousse

¾ quart whipping cream
⅓ quart milk
½ vanilla bean
1 tablespoon plus 1 teaspoon ground coffee
¼ cup plus 3 tablespoons granulated sugar
2¼ gelatin sheets
4½ egg yolks
1¾ cup melted bittersweet chocolate

Whip cream to soft peaks. Bring milk, vanilla, coffee, and half the sugar to a boil. Let infuse for 10 minutes. Soften gelatin sheets in cold water. Add to the milk mixture. Cream egg yolks and then very slowly add the milk/gelatin mixture to create a crème anglaise. Strain the crème anglaise through a fine-mesh china cap. Add melted chocolate to crème anglaise, return to mixer bowl, and stir till cold. The chocolate mixture will thicken. Incorporate chocolate mixture into whipped cream, pour over the cakes and refrigerate overnight.

Courtesy of Pastry Chef Mindy Reed, Zin American Bistro

ONE OF CHEF PIERRE PELECH'S MOST POPULAR DESSERTS is this adaptation of a contemporary French classic.

BAKED THIN APPLE TART

Serves four

1 sheet puff pastry, frozen
1 Granny Smith apple, peeled,
  cored, and sliced thin
2 tablespoons sugar
1 teaspoon cinnamon
1½ cups vanilla ice cream

Cut an 8-inch circle in the puff pastry and place on a jellyroll pan. Lay apple on pastry puff 1 inch from the side, sprinkle the sugar over the apples, and bake at 375°F for about 10 minutes. Then remove the tart from the oven and sprinkle the cinnamon over it. Cut the tart into four pieces. Place each piece on a dessert plate and finish by topping it off with a scoop of ice cream.

Courtesy of Chef Pierre Pelech,
Chez Pierre Bistro

DESERT BREAD PUDDING

Makes one pan

10 egg yolks
⅔ cup granulated sugar
1 vanilla bean, split
4 cups heavy cream
1 cup whole milk
3 tablespoons spiced rum

4 cups brioche or challah bread,
cubed
1½ cups dates
1½ cups dried apricots
1½ cups dried figs, small or diced
Confectioner's sugar

Preheat the oven to 350°F. Lightly butter a standard loaf pan. Set a large bowl into a larger bowl of ice. In a medium bowl whisk the egg yolks and sugar until the mixture looks creamy, then add rum. Scrape the seeds from the center of the vanilla bean and add it to a medium pan (add the pod, to be removed later). Add cream and milk to pan and heat to boiling. Add a small amount of the hot milk and cream to the yolk mixture to liquify it a bit, then reduce heat to medium and slowly stir in the yolk/sugar mixture. Cook, stirring constantly, until mixture coats spoon (or spatula), being careful not to let the mixture boil.

Remove from heat and pour through a strainer into the bowl set in ice and chill until just warm. Put the bread into a large bowl and add just enough of the warm cream to coat and soak the bread. It should be like a very wet sponge; there may be some cooked cream left. Layer the bread, followed by the mixed fruits, then the bread and fruit again. The top layer is the creamy bread.

Cook the pudding in a *bain-marie*, a loaf pan set into a baking pan filled with about an inch of water. Cook for 60 minutes until a sharp knife inserted in the center comes out clean. Cool to room temperature and then refrigerate. When completely chilled, turn upside down and remove from loaf pan.

TO SERVE
Slice into 1-inch pieces, then line the pieces up on a cookie sheet. Sprinkle each slice with confectioner's sugar and caramelize under the broiler. Use a large spatula to move slice to center of the dessert plate.

Courtesy of Pastry Chef Laurent Dellac, Le Vallauris Restaurant

Chef's Tip

Serve with rum raisin ice cream and crème anglaise.

SWEET CREPES WITH VANILLA-SAUTÉED STRAWBERRIES

Makes four servings of two crepes each

Sweet Crepes

¾ cup flour
2 tablespoons sugar
1 teaspoon salt
1 cup milk
2 eggs
1 tablespoon melted butter
½ teaspoon vanilla
2 tablespoons melted butter for cooking
Vanilla-Sautéed Strawberries, recipe follows

Whisk together the flour, sugar, and salt in a medium bowl. Gradually whisk in the milk, then the eggs, one at a time, then the melted butter and vanilla. Cover and chill in the refrigerator for one hour. Place a 10-inch nonstick skillet or crepe pan over medium-high heat. Brush the skillet with melted butter to lightly coat the surface.

Ladle about ¼ cup of batter into the pan and move the ladle in a circular pattern to coat the pan with a thin, even layer of batter. Cook for 2 minutes until the first side browns very lightly and edges are dry. Flip the crepe and cook about 1 minute longer. Remove to a baking sheet or plate and repeat with remaining batter, brushing the pan lightly with butter and stacking the crepes as they finish.

To serve the crepes warm, preheat the oven to its lowest setting. Place the sheet with the stacked cooked crepes, covered with foil, in the oven to keep them warm. The crepes can also be made in advance, stacked on a plate, covered with plastic wrap, and refrigerated. Bring the crepes to room temperature or warm them before serving.

Continued on next page

Vanilla-Sautéed Strawberries

2 cups fresh strawberries
1 vanilla bean
2 tablespoons butter
2–3 teaspoons sugar, to taste

Juice of ½ lemon
Maple syrup for topping
Freshly whipped cream for topping

Hull the strawberries and cut each into bite-size pieces. Place a medium nonstick skillet over medium heat. Cut the vanilla bean in two and scrape out the seeds from half of the bean with a small paring knife, saving the other half for another use. Melt the butter in the skillet, add the vanilla seeds and strawberry pieces, and stir gently to coat the strawberries with the butter. Sprinkle the sugar over the strawberries and stir in gently, adjusting sugar to taste. Sauté for 2–3 minutes until berries begin to soften, being careful not to overcook, then remove from heat. Add a small squirt of lemon juice, giving the mixture a final stir.

TO SERVE
Place two crepes on a plate. Then top half of each crepe with a spoonful of the warm strawberries and a bit of the sauce from the pan, and fold over the other halves of the crepes. Serve immediately. You may choose to garnish the crepes with a small dribble of maple syrup. If serving as a dessert, place a dollop of freshly whipped cream on the side.

Courtesy of Chef Karen Stiegler

Chef's Tip

This is a great recipe for breakfast, brunch, or dessert! These crepes are cooked on both sides until they are a light golden brown—the vanilla and two eggs give the crepes wonderful flavor and aroma. The berries are lightly sautéed in vanilla and butter until they are soft on the outside but al dente in the center.

Choose brightly colored strawberries that still have their green caps attached and are as red as possible—berries with whitish areas on top or bottom may not be fully ripened. The real test of ripeness is when you bite into a strawberry; the center should also be completely red. The flavor of smaller berries is usually better than that of larger strawberries. Fresh strawberries are available year-round in many regions of the country, with peak season from April to June. Do not wash your berries until you are ready to use them; store them in a moisture-proof container in the refrigerator for two to three days.

La Quinta Lemon Bars

Crust

2 cups flour
½ cup sugar
¼ teaspoon salt

½ cup butter, unsalted
¼ cup shortening

Filling

1 cup sugar
3 tablespoons flour
2 eggs, slightly beaten
½ cup water

1 tablespoon lemon zest
½ cup lemon juice
2 tablespoons butter, unsalted

Glaze

½ cup powdered sugar
1 tablespoon whole milk

Preheat oven to 375°F. To make crust, combine flour, sugar, and salt. Using a pastry blender, cut butter and shortening into the dry mixture until the particles are fine. Reserve one cup. Press the remainder into an ungreased 9 by 3-inch pan and bake for 12 minutes. To prepare the filling, combine flour and sugar in a saucepan, then stir in all the remaining ingredients. Cook over medium-high heat, stirring constantly until very thick. Spread filling over baked crust and sprinkle with reserved crumbs. Combine powdered sugar and milk for glaze and drizzle on top. Bake 20–25 minutes longer. When cool, cut into small bars.

Courtesy of Chef Eric Wadlund, Beefsteak Restaurant

ABOUT THE AUTHORS & PHOTOGRAPHER

HENRY FENWICK began his career as a book, theatre, and film critic in London. He was imported to the USA by *Playboy* magazine, where he temporarily became an expert on American sex laws and mores. Returning to London, he joined the BBC as the features and planning editor for its weekly magazine *Radio Times*, the BBC equivalent of *TV Guide*. He later freelanced in New York, writing for the *New York Times*, the BBC, the *London Times*, *Esquire*, and many others.

After moving to Los Angeles, Henry became editor of *Modern Maturity*, and led a highly acclaimed redesign with New York designers Walter Bernard and Milton Glaser.

When the magazine moved to Washington, D.C., he supervised the move, then returned to California. He came to the desert to rethink, rename, and redesign the monthly magazine published by the *Desert Sun*, now titled *Desert Magazine*. After the redesign was implemented and set securely on its way, he left the *Desert Sun* to write about food, which has been a lifelong interest. He has a regular food column in the *Desert Sun* and in *Desert Magazine*.

ERIC WADLUND is the co-owner and chef of Beefsteak, in Rancho Mirage. Eric started cooking when he was four; his father owned a bakery in Wisconsin. His first creation: donuts. He quickly learned how very, very popular you can be if you can produce food for your friends. His culinary career began when he served as an apprentice at the Madison Club in Wisconsin. He then went on to work at the Occidental Restaurant, next to the White House in Washington, D.C. Eric became executive chef at Café Terra Cotta in Tucson, Arizona, which was named one of the Top Ten Bistros in the United States by the American Academy of Restaurants and Hospitality Sciences. He and his wife Rowena went on to open Rio Grill in Tucson.

In the Coachella Valley, Wadlund was also executive chef and director of operations at Rattlesnake, Chef Jimmy Schmidt's showplace restaurant in the Spotlight 29 Casino. He left there to become chef de cuisine at Azur by Le Bernardin, located at the La Quinta Resort and Club, then became Azur's executive chef when the Le Bernardin connection ended. He and Rowena opened Beefsteak in the fall of 2006.

TONY TORNAY was born on the East Coast but moved to the Palm Springs area when he was 6 years old. After graduating from Palm Desert High School in 1991, he attended Art Center College of Design in Pasadena, California, where he earned a Bachelor of Arts in Photography. Since graduation he has been busy shooting for the entertainment industry and numerous magazines, while continuing to work on his own personal body of work. His work has appeared on numerous record albums (and subsequent advertising campaigns) along with magazines such as *Rolling Stone*, *Flaunt*, *Unleashed*, *Tidbit*, and *Desert Magazine*, among others. Tony now divides his time between Los Angeles and Palm Desert.